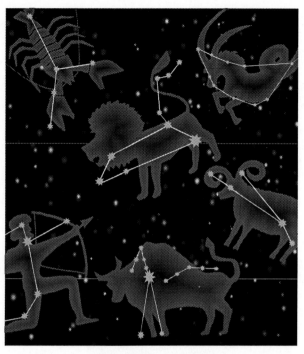

ZODIAC

INSPIRATIONS -
A COLLECTION OF
INTERNATIONAL POETS

Edited by Lynsey Hawkins

First published in Great Britain in 2002 by
YOUNG WRITERS
Remus House,
Coltsfoot Drive,
Peterborough, PE2 9JX, UK
Telephone (01733) 890066

HB ISBN 0 75433 640 9
SB ISBN 0 75433 641 7

FOREWORD

Young Writers was established in 1991 with the aim of promoting creative writing in children, to make reading and writing poetry fun.

The Zodiac competition has shown us the high standard of work and effort that children are capable of today. The competition has given us a vivid insight into the thoughts and experiences of today's younger generation. It is a reflection of the enthusiasm and creativity that teachers have injected into their pupils, and it shines clearly within this anthology.

The task of selecting poems was a difficult one, but nevertheless, an enjoyable experience. We hope you are as pleased with the final selection in *Zodiac Inspirations - A Collection Of International Poets* as we are.

CONTENTS

The Poems

MAMA YOU HAVE CRIED

Mama, you have cried a river of tears longer than
the Nile River and deeper than the occupying oceans.
Your life is more than an autobiography of man's trials and
tribulations on the quest to define the meaning of mixed emotions.
Mama, you have cried a night of many dreams, a world of
                                             unbearable fears,
a symphony of screams through a soul that constantly bleeds.
You wish to knock upon the door of eternity and never return
to what used to be and to what never should have been.
You have been strong enough to overwhelm the Devil and
have managed to weaken his forsaken deeds,
yet are weak enough to let go of the happiness that grasps your hand
leading you to the land of the free.
Mama you have cried tears enough to sink Mount Kilimanjaro and
drown the sins of this cruel world, but through all the misery
you have never forgotten that I am your black pearl.
When your heart ends its journey of despair, it is only then
will you realise that your first daughter has always been there.
Having always thought that you were alone in this world,
where life goes on, leaving the slow behind and heading for the future
without realising that not looking back isn't fair,
you forever staying strong and bold enough to reveal your Kaffir hair.
Mama, now you smile for the overly depressed and have learned
to live, even for the dead, now I can close my eyes and imagine us
dancing on the purple hills of Madagascar and lie
the sadness away on a heavenly flower bed.
You will never remember the tears you cried because jubilation has
your memories dried up in winds of your freedom.
Mama, you cry no more; Mama, you fear no more;
Mama you die no more because now, you live for four.

Lonwabokazi Happiness Mkuyana
American School of Madrid

I Could Go On Like This Forever

The thudding of the bass
Cuts through conversations like a knife
The night air is filled with rhythm
Running through everyone's warm blood
A rhythm that could never cease

Bodies press up hard against me
Hands, fingers, arms, legs, exploring all of me
The crowd swallowing me alive
The music forces everyone to dance
Elbows fly for their own inch of space

Every part of me glistens with cool sweat
It drips into my eyes and mouth
A salty taste that stings my eyes
My hair flies wild in the star-filled sky
And for a moment I am blinded

Through the crowd I see a dark stranger
Who is staring and pushing his way through towards me
He grabs my face and screams something into my ear
What are you saying?
But then again, who really cares?

My body throbs all over
Inhaling the smoke makes my throat burn
The alcohol churns and gurgles in my stomach
Another song blasts into my pounding head
I could go on like this forever . . .

René Benavídez (18)
American School of Madrid

Untitled

My
boundaries are
stenciled
for my life it seems.
Not to put one step out is
what I'm told and seen,

because only ones
who have, have
lived their lives
through
dreams.

Valerie Skeete
American School of Madrid

WINTER!

Taste -
The cold air and the snow
Which hits your face
And quickly turns into water.

Hear -
The wind whining and
The trees slowly moving
Back and forth.

Smell -
The evergreen trees and
The newly baked cookies.

See -
The naked tress and the snow
Which covers all of the land.

Touch -
The freezing snow with your hands
And the warm feeling of a
Cup of hot chocolate.

Vincent Myers (13)
Bladin's International School, Sweden

BEACH

See -
> the waves meeting each other
> as they crash together and back again.
> The tidal waves splashing against
> the sandy shore.

Touch -
> the soft and dry sand which
> softly slips out of your hands,
> wet on one side of the shore
> and dry on the other.

Taste -
> of the seaweed
> invades your mouth
> as you inhale the sea air.

Smell -
> the seaweed,
> the salty water,
> the smell comes and goes.

Hear -
> the seagulls cawing
> while they're looking for food.

Pia Gogia (14)
Bladin's International School, Sweden

SENSES

Taste -
Chocolate pudding in my mouth;
The coolness of the air;
The taste of ashes.

Hear -
Children outside;
Playing with snowballs;
Dad bringing in the Christmas tree;
Cars skidding on the ice outside.

Smell -
The gingerbread being baked in the oven;
My grandmother next to me;
My newly bought book.

See -
Children making snowmen outside;
The snowballs being thrown;
The text in my book.

Touch -
The spiky Christmas tree;
The back cover of my book;
The warmth of the fire on my skin.

Ivar Sahlqvist (13)
Bladin's International School, Sweden

DECEMBER SENSES

Taste -
The Christmas buns, sweet,
And cookies crunching between teeth.
Hot chocolate sweeping down throats,
Giving a warm taste of comfort.

Hear -
Carols through the streets,
Crackling fireplaces,
Sounds of laughter, church bells,
Choir and breaking Christmas decorations.

Smell -
Mothers and daughters baking,
The cinnamon smells pouring out of the ovens.
Fathers and their sons bring in the pine trees,
As fireplaces through the neighbourhoods,
Bring in smells of winter ash and smoke.

See -
The children throwing snowballs,
And making their snowmen big and tall.
Flakes are falling,
Looking like swarms of white wasps if you look up.

Touch -
Cuddling in front of the fireplace.
Being lifted by your father's strong hands,
To put up the Christmas star.
Rubbing your arms to get warm.

Sophie Roest (13)
Bladin's International School, Sweden

GREEN

Green is like a necklace
with emeralds all over it.
It is the sound of the greenish spit
of an old pirate falling on the floor,
and the smell of fresh grass on top of the hill
that cures you if you're ill.
It is the sound of the wind
running between the trees and touching
the moisty leaves from a tree
next to a waterfall.
But that's not all.
It is also the fresh mint that you put under your nose
with no other purpose than to smell it.
That is green.

Fernando Silvestre Rubio (12)
Colegio Hispano-Norteamericano, Valencia

JANUARY

The flowers are hidden so they can be warm
You are an angry and furious man
Who makes cold and damp weather
As I amble through the street
I wither in my clothes
Your friend, the freezing, unfriendly wind
Tries to get at my neck
And make me shiver,
But the thick, cozy scarf protects my vulnerable throat
Although you are so uncomfortable,
I love to be sleeping in my bed and covering myself
With a bunch of warm and comfortable blankets.

Carmen Gimeno Vilarrasa (13)
Colegio Hispano-Norteamericano, Valencia

HAPPINESS

Happiness is like perfume
That slowly extends throughout the people.
Happiness is a world full of peace and love,
In a world without hunger and wars
There wouldn't be any more children
In the poor countries crying for some food,
While in the rich countries,
People have everything they want
And keep asking for more.

Happiness is Christmas
When all the family gets together.
It's a time of peace and love.
The streets are full of decorations:
Colorful lights, Christmas trees sprinkled with round stars.
Santa with his white beard, like a fluffy cloud.

Happiness is when my soccer team wins
And the stadium roars with enthusiasm.

Happiness is a mother's expression
When her baby is born.

Happiness is like a small creature that creeps
Into our hearts and lights the world around us.

Antonio Tormo Sáez-Merino (12)
Colegio Hispano-Norteamericano, Valencia

AUTUMN

Autumn, you are an old man
sitting lonely, talking to the cold forest,
wondering how the wrinkling,
mixed red and yellow leaves fall
like drops from a cloud,
not caring how the landing is going to be.

Autumn, you are a tiny piece of corn
in a curious field with a red sky and no clouds,
you are an unhappy orange pumpkin,
perching on the window of a lonely house
in a lonely forest.

Marc Sanjuan Jubert (13)
Colegio Hispano-Norteamericano, Valencia

CLEOPATRA VII

Oh you romantic friend,
You were so in trend.
You were the leader
And such a good reader.
Oh you romantic friend,
You were so in trend.
First with Julius,
The boy came out so curious,
Then with Mark,
He had such a knack,
But you couldn't with Octavian,
He was a barbarian.
Oh you romantic friend,
You were so in trend,
But the poisonous asp
Wasn't the last
To get to your breast.
Oh you romantic friend,
You were so in trend.

Ana Díez Gandía (13)
Colegio Hispano-Norteamericano, Valencia

DEAR MOM

Dear Mom, dear Mom!
Thanks for all the courage that you've had,
Showed us, for all that courage you had,
Had when Dad went.

Dear Mom, dear Mom!
I want to thank you that when all
Was a complete disaster,
You never went down.

Dear Mom, dear Mom!
Thanks, for when I felt blue and blind,
You gave me love and helped me find the star.

Dear Mom, dear Mom!
I think that you are the highest woman
That I will ever know,
Because when we need your help
We will always find your heart
And when I need you, there you are.

Thanks Mom, thanks Mom!
Sometimes you were like my boat
In a deep, blue, solitary, huge, immense ocean,
But finally I will find heaven
And I will be always by your side.

Patricia Fernández-Déniz (13)
Colegio Hispano-Norteamericano, Valencia

EMBARRASSED

My face turns pink, then purple, then red,
I would rather sink instead.
Nibbling nervously my nails,
Suddenly, I turn pale!
My tongue covered with a sticky glue,
Like the amber resin that picks me and you.
I can't talk, not even a world,
I can only hear the singing of a bird.
I feel everyone staring and laughing at me,
I feel sweat rolling down from my forehead to my chin.
I am really hot,
Like a cooking pot.
My heart pounds in my chest,
Like robins fighting on their nest.
I want to close my eyes and sleep,
Dreaming with white, cotton sheep.

Ana Mercado Bayona (12)
Colegio Hispano-Norteamericano, Valencia

FEAR

Fear, the feeling you have when you are scared
The feeling you have when you see someone dead.
Fear is an enigmatical, bulky nightmare
That we all unfortunately share.
You think that you hear voices,
But that is all imagination noises.
Fear is squeaking doors
And mysterious creaking floors.
You see faces vanishing through the air
And some people ask themselves . . .
Will this terror finish some day?

Albert Amigó Agustí (13)
Colegio Hispano-Norteamericano, Valencia

STARS

We the stars,
Dressed with a tunic
Of needles
With our silver eyes,
Observing the sleep of humans.

We the stars,
Strolling around in the dark
With a tail of glitter.

We the stars,
Those sparkling, brilliant dots
Above the night sky.

We the stars,
Disappear when
The sun shows off
Her wonderful
Blonde hair.

We the stars,
Are there to
Make your wishes
Come true when
You ask for them.

We the stars,
Are here to
Dress up
The sky.

Elisa Gómez Monzó (12)
Colegio Hispano-Norteamericano, Valencia

CINEMA

Bright, full of light,
But all of a sudden it becomes night.
Loud, hard, blasting noise,
The interesting, exciting, scary movie begins . . .
You are there all alone . . .
Slowly sipping a cool, chilled Coke.
Nice and comfy in a smooth, cosy seat,
Enjoying your hot, buttery popcorn treat.
All of a sudden . . .
Ahhh!
People start screaming
And you start shivering.
You can't watch any more murders,
You'd rather go for some juicy beef burgers.

Chaya Chugani (13)
Colegio Hispano-Norteamericano, Valencia

LIFE

Life, life, life,
There are different faces in life.
Sometimes it is as sour as a lime,
Sometimes as sweet as the strawberry which is sublime.
How you want to live your life you decide,
Love your work, like your life and don't leave anything for tomorrow.
Life, life, life, strange vacation till you die.
Try to be happy and try to smile every day and every moment
Because we are not cats, we only have one life.
It's easier to live the life you live but . . .
It's better to live the life you like.

Lucia Ribes Clerigues (14)
Colegio Hispano-Norteamericano, Valencia

LIFE

Labyrinth, a green, large labyrinth,
you have to make a decision,
there are too many ways.
Sometimes you will decide a way,
but you could reach a dead end and
you will have to start again.
While you walk, the flower's smell
enters your nose and it makes you feel calm,
you know you are in the right way,
maybe walking through the rain a sun will appear
and no night will exist.
You walk, making your own decisions,
but some will take you to a bad life
and some to a good life,
so that when you reach that labyrinth,
stop, look at it and decide where you want to go.
Life: an amazing thing.

Laura Guinot Ruiz (13)
Colegio Hispano-Norteamericano, Valencia

LONELINESS

Loneliness is hard work in the bin.
It's not a nice feeling.
It's like a gigantic field,
Void of flowers.
But only one was there
In the center, alone,
Without any friends,
Without a blanket
That will protect her.

That flower is now dead.
Nobody knows because
She was alone in life,
Alone in a field,
Alone in the
Middle of the night.

Paula Traver Martin (12)
Colegio Hispano-Norteamericano, Valencia

ME, A CANDLE

I'm the forgotten familiar,
Only called when help is needed.

When gloominess comes,
I also appear.

Once my life starts,
My death is initiated.

Ploddingly and steadily I die,
Unhurriedly, my life consumes.

My body, once fine and lofty, melts
And my golden hair attends my body, vanishing.

My life now has ended
And I'm a frozen puddle.

Now brightness comes
And, who remembers me?

Maria José Sala Peluffo (13)
Colegio Hispano-Norteamericano, Valencia

RAIN

Rain doesn't always wet floors.
It wrecks people's dresses.
Rain runs rapidly through the street
And flies in the air.
It makes people slip.

Rain doesn't always make
A flood.
It tells you where
The ceiling broke.

Rain doesn't always wet cars.
It wakes up the snails when they are snoring
And makes trees grow when they are thirsty.
Rain can be fast, frightening,
And cold like ice.
Rain is someone you have to live with.

Juan Vázquez Díez (12)
Colegio Hispano-Norteamericano, Valencia

SUN

The sun is a lemon
at 12:00 noon.
A yellow balloon
flying slowly.

A big, hot ball
angrily blowing in my face
making me red.
The father of
nine children.

The sun is like an
orange in the dusk.
The sun leaves slowly
and silently from the sky
and I say farewell, goodbye!

Adrian Gimenez (12)
Colegio Hispano-Norteamericano, Valencia

CHRISTMAS TREE

Surrounded by friends,
Home, sweet home,
All covered with chilly snow
Christmas is closer.

Christmas is here,
Families come to take us
Out of our house.

My delightful white dress melts
With the heat of the fire.
I saw I was a beautiful green.

The happy family
Dressed me with balls and candles
And surround me with presents.

One sad day,
The happy family
Threw me in the middle
Of a dead wood.

There slowly, silently,
My clothing went brown
And I died of thirst.

Celia Baviera Palencia (13)
Colegio Hispano-Norteamericano, Valencia

SPRING

Your name means color, happiness.
When you arrive, everybody sings,
Everybody dances and everything blooms.
You are a nymph gambolling around
The green and mysterious forest.
The rays of sun that appear
Through the gigantic trees,
Make your curly hair
Look as thin layers of gold.
From the end of that intangible hair,
Little sparkles of pollen
Are dispersed all around
And your eyes look like two drops of dew,
The first dawn of spring.

Beatriz Gimeno Vilarrasa (13)
Colegio Hispano-Norteamericano, Valencia

SUNRISE

The sky is purplish-blue,
now has passed the morning dew.
Orange, yellow and then red,
is the sun when you're in bed.
From the rooftop, from the gables,
caws the rooster, between the cables.
The bells in the steeple
awaken the people.
Birds softly flying,
the night peacefully dying.
The big, orange sunrise
is like an old man who is wise.

Alba Trullenque Pardo (13)
Colegio Hispano-Norteamericano, Valencia

GREAT GRANDMOTHER

Dear Great Grandmother,
Oh, how I loved you.
You were as vulnerable
As a baby.
You were kilometres away but that didn't matter,
Because I remembered you as if you were here.
When I went to see you,
You were always showing us
How you were when you were younger.
You gave us presents
And now I contemplate them.
You were always sitting in your
Small, dark and smooth chair.
Suddenly, when our grandparents were going to come,
You closed your eyes and disappeared forever.

Martín Estrela Jiménez (13)
Colegio Hispano-Norteamericano, Valencia

SNOW

Snow is like
Many shimmering,
Silver shivers.
Snow speaks
Of a sad, soft tale.
It sings
A silent, swaying song.
Snow is a large swan
Sailing through the air,
Shattering into thousands
Of swirling, small seagulls.

Marina Pinilla (12)
Colegio Hispano-Norteamericano, Valencia

MY AUNT

My aunt is the person I most love in the world
'cause she is always there
when I most need her,
and little by little,
without letting me know,
she was becoming the person I love the most.
My aunt is marvellous,
she is also crazy,
but she is one of the best things that has
ever happened to me, ever.
She also is one of the prettiest women
I have ever seen.
People say that is because I love her a lot
and it's true,
'cause she would listen to me for
whatever I have to say.
My aunt isn't marvellous only,
she is also elegant and beautiful
and a lot of adjectives more,
but she is so splendid and pretty
that there wouldn't be enough adjectives
to describe a person like my aunt.
Because of that and a lot more things,
I have decided something,
when I grow up and have a job,
the person I want to spend the rest of my days with
is my aunt.
The best aunt you could ever devise,
that one is my aunt,
Pilar.

María Segarra Querol (13)
Colegio Hispano-Norteamericano, Valencia

LIFE

Life,
life is a blanket,
an endless blanket,
a blanket of miles and miles of strings,
all sorts of strings,
blue and green,
thick and thin,
strings that criss-cross in different directions,
full of confusions,
confusions of love and hate,
full of complications,
in work and diseases,
full of decisions,
decisions of whether taking one or another.

Life,
life is a candle.
It is born with a light,
a smooth and shiny light.
When it is happy it rises,
rises up as high as it can,
and when it's depressed,
it sinks right down,
low, very low,
and then it dies,
when the fire is gone,
gone forever,
until the next life comes.

Jenny A Carlsson (12)
Colegio Hispano-Norteamericano, Valencia

YELLOW

I have a problem,
My problem is called Yellow.

She is so false,
She never feels what she says.

She's pathetic!

She tries to copy all of us:

She wants to be
As explosive as Red,
As friendly as Orange.

Even tries to copy me,
But she won't
Be as original as me, Purple.

She tries to be
As smart as White,
As elegant as Gold and
As cool as Silver.

But she is set,
She's just Yellow,
A simple colour
With not a bit of personality.

Marta Verdú Ramírez (13)
Colegio Hispano-Norteamericano, Valencia

TERROR ON AMERICA

I was working normally
Like any other day
On the 100th floor
Knowing not what was on its way
At 8:40
My work was done
As I was leaving
From Tower One
Then I remembered
I'd forgotten my case
I went back in,
But it had vanished without a trace
Suddenly, the building shakes
My head hits the desk
And my glasses break
Underneath me, voices I hear
It's quite faint,
But still it is near
As I pick up my glasses to look around
I look out of the window
People were falling
Down to the ground
Instead of facing the wild flame
I make my choice
I jump, for the flames will roar untamed
I open the window, I jump
I fly down, down, then . . .

Stephen Lyssejko & Danny Seelen (12)
Ecole Européenne, Luxembourg

LADY PEINFORTE'S SEARCH FOR THE COMET, NEMESIS

There once was a lady called Peinforte,
Who had a fine henchman whom she'd bought.
The lady was armed with a bow,
She shot, but she just missed a crow.
The crow was a target she'd picked
And the henchman didn't wish to be kicked,
'Very good, m'lady,' was all he said,
For he did want his daily bread.
Lady Peinforte at this simply scowled,
And with fury she practically howled.
They went back inside when the birds had stopped cooing,
To see how the mathematician was doing.

He said, 'I have worked out the orbit!'
She asked, 'Are you sure you have got it?'
'The comet is flying, or so it appears,
It circles the Earth every twenty-five years.
In the year of our Lord, nineteen-eighty-eight,
It will land in the meadow behind your back gate.'
'Is the potion ready, what more can it need?'
'It requires human blood!' said Richard with greed.
He killed the poor scientist and took all his blood,
When they drank the potion, it tasted like mud.

They travelled through time, for three hundred years,
And poor Richard, he almost burst into tears.
They were in a tea shop, in the very same place,
And a police car was driving at a tremendous pace.
T'was looking for Nemesis, the comet they sought,
What kind of carriage is that? Richard thought.
They leapt out of a window and ran to the crash site,
Lady Peinforte then shouted, 'Beware the comet's might!'

The lady, who was mad, jumped on to the rock,
It blasted back into space, the man got a shock.
The potion wore off, Richard was glad,
The lady did not return, but that was not sad.

Philip Wickens (12)
Ecole Européenne, Luxembourg

MY POEM!

I've this poem to write,
much to my delight.

I asked my dad to assist,
but there's a bit of a twist.

Today is a Tuesday,
not a good news day.

For this poem, my delight,
must be written by tonight.

It's a competition
and you'll supply the ammunition.

With punctuation and dictation,
this poem may be my ruination.

The final destination
for my imagination

Is a generous donation
to my place of education.

Macdara Spaine (12)
Ecole Européenne, Luxembourg

A SECOND OF HAPPINESS

A shining smile filled her face,
A face belonging to a lady,
A lady of beauty.
Her hair was pulled back into a respectable bun,
Her brand new suit was smartly pressed
And her shoes glistened in the sparkling sunlight.
She walked down her road,
Around the corner,
Towards a new life.
A *new* life,
New work,
Meeting new people,
Finding her one true love
She squinted as the tall tower came into view
Reflecting sun into her gleaming eyes.
She marched towards it,
Her shoes clapping against the hard stone floor
Her destiny lay before her.
Her office was on floor 95,
Small, but ideal for her.
She unpacked her photos
Of happy memories and times,
They were with her wherever she went.
Settling down into her black revolving chair,
Leaning back to look at all the minute people
Scurrying about on Earth
She thought how lucky she was to be alive
The floor shuddered,
Photos dropped, glass shattered, screams echoed
A twinge of panic ran up her spine,
She shivered and stared out of the window,
All she could see was dust, endless dust and flames.

She gasped at the horrific image and closed her blinds hurriedly
Running out of her office to the lifts,
Pushing her way through swarms of puzzled colleagues
She found out what was going on,
A plane had crashed into the building.
People scampered down the stairs trying to escape the disaster.
She, on the other hand,
Retreated to her office,
The ground was hot,
Papers fluttered around her anxious face,
Smoke and dust were appearing out of tiny cracks in the walls
She sat down in her chair surrounded by
Her family and closed her eyes
Remembering how happy she had been an hour ago
And now it was all over.
The smoke was intruding into her office;
It surrounded her in a swift gulp
The flames were licking at the doorframe.
She could barely see the corridor,
But what she did see brought tears to her eyes.
Mothers, fathers, lovers, ringing desperately on
Their mobiles to contact their treasured ones,
Choking on every word they muttered,
The flames devouring their feet as they fell to the ground.
Never to see the world again
Never to breathe the same air
Or hear the sweet voices of their children
Telling them how much they loved them.
She pulled open her blinds and flung open the window
Trying to savour the last breaths of air and life.
Bodies were falling from the sky as if escaping a floundering ship
Tears were cascading from her eyes,
Death was on its way,
But there was always hope.

In a flash,
There was no more screaming,
No more pain and aching,
Just empty numbness filled her flaccid body.
She could no longer hear the tormenting bawls of the innocent
She was away with the angels.
She had been happy for a second.

Laura Marshall (12)
Ecole Européenne, Luxembourg

DAEDALUS AND ICARUS

I make a labyrinth for Minos.
Nobody can possibly escape,
But big, bad Theseus gets out.

Me and my son are brought into the labyrinth.
We get stale bread and water to eat and drink
And a thin mattress to sleep on.

My son makes friends with the bees and birds.
I ask him to collect feathers from the birds,
I ask him to collect wax from the bees.
I use them to make wings for me and my son.

My son and I fly away,
My son flies too close to the sun,
My son falls into the sea.
I fly sadly on to Sicily, crying as I go.

Claire Macklin (12)
Ecole Européenne, Luxembourg

TO THINK OF IT . . .

To think of it, how lucky we are,
Still alive.
Thousands of lives buried beneath the debris and rubble.
To think of it, how painful it was,
We could not save the helpless souls.
The thought of the ill-fated fall was chilling,
How I wished it was nothing but a movie.
The thought of the screams and tears in the air,
The rescuers were there, but gone with the fall.
However, the touch of happiness has now vanished,
Let's keep vigil round a candle,
When shaken by recent tragedies,
When overcome by daily worries.

Alizaeh Mahmood (11)
Ecole Européenne, Luxembourg

AN AUTUMN IN LUXEMBOURG

I looked around on an autumn day.
Leaves were falling from their trees,
Swirling and dancing on their way
Until they touched the ground without a sound.
They looked like fireworks in daytime,
But without disappearing,
When you looked on the ground there they were.
After one or two months later, the trees were bare
And there was a chill in the air.
Everywhere you looked was white,
Then you knew winter had come
And you would have to wait until spring
To see another leaf.

Cillian Spillane (11)
Ecole Européenne, Luxembourg

HORROR, PANIC, DEATH

It was a sunny day
As I walked to work.
Another normal day,
Same people, same friends.

I got into the elevator,
Puzzling about stocks.
Another normal day,
Same people, same friends.

I sat down at my desk
And started to work.
Another normal day,
Same people, same friends.

A while later, a big *thud* occurred.
People shouting, people screaming.
I looked out of the window; things were falling.
People shouting, people screaming.

In my mind, my life, my family.
People shouting, people screaming.
I looked for the stairs, in horror, in panic.
People shouting, people screaming.

Out! Out! My only thought.
Standing there, paralysed.
Watching the buildings disappear.
All silent. No people. No friends.

Jascha Eisenberg (12)
Ecole Européenne, Luxembourg

I COULD HAVE NOT

I could have not been here,
I could have been gone,
If I hadn't looked to the right at the crossing,
Then turned to the left,
Simple things like this
Serve for a purpose.
A single move could have changed your life.

I could have not noticed him,
I could have walked on
And my life would have been different,
Simple like all.
A single person could have changed your life.

It could have been killed,
The yellow daffodil,
If my mum had not told me
Not to pick flowers.
A simple snip could have killed one's soul!

Now I understand
What small movements do.
Now I understand
What a simple glance could do.
A simple thought,
A simple move,
A second thought
Could do much more than you think it could do.

Jasmine Wong (11)
Ecole Européenne, Luxembourg

AUTUMN FAIRIES

It's been six years,
Almost to the day,
When I watched you dance with the leaves.
And then the people came,
Beautiful, they entranced you,
Those Dancing Fairies of Autumn.

But you were only young,
Then my head turned away,
But when I turned back
You were nowhere to be seen,
You had gone,
With those Dancing Fairies of Autumn.

I went out one autumn night
And there was dancing
With the leaves,
A beautiful child,
Naked, but gold hair rolls over shoulders,
A Dancing Fairy of Autumn.

And then she turns to me,
As I watch the magic,
I look into her face
And my child stands before me,
Not the round girl with brown hair,
But a Dancing Fairy of Autumn.

Clare McGing (12)
Ecole Européenne, Luxembourg

VALEDICTION

Death tempted me with a kiss,
Relieved me from the burden of life,
Enveloped me in pure bliss,
Removed my melancholy and strife.

Loved ones: do not be distraught,
My friends: for me, do not weep.
I found the peace which I sought:
Heavenly, eternal sleep.

Natasha Marks (15)
Ecole Européenne, Luxembourg

SONG OF THE BROTHEL

There chimes no tock, no gong, no bell
To spell the challenging tide of hours
When from themselves they come, running.
But come they do, sad cockroaches hither
To the wenching docks, with coins
To take their stock of lovers true
And handsome as the bribe-silver
Being passed along the line.
My girls of sunning, raven hair, of copper
Deeper than their burnished coins,
Do what they've lain waiting all day to do:
The creatures guilten brazenly and gold
Shall pay for that pretty gilt sin.
Oh but wake me at the witching hour
To taste their salty skins together,
Each unique innocent screaming 'Brother!'
At her final duty -
And I, their sister-by, but a consonant lonely
From their mingled cry.

Rose Edwards (15)
Ecole Européenne, Luxembourg

REPRIEVE

Bright midday sun shines through the window.
Rays catch the objects on the floor.
They leak shadows.

Cast, they skip across the ground,
But fail to hide the tin soldier who has just stood up.
He blinks; *what is this place?*

But he has been lost for some time now
And reflects with simmering hysteria
One more place to be lost in hardly matters.

Perhaps this is heaven?
It surely isn't hell.
He'd just woken from that place, from Pandemonium.

Chaos and the thud of shells,
Spatters of blood and stuttering machine gun fire.
In war, everyone is deaf.

In war everyone is dead
Or shell shocked and waiting to die.
A sparrow chirps outside,
Pulling him out of the bomb crater he was drowning in.

There are people and amazing creatures lying still.
He wanders through the battlefield of scattered toys.
He does not recognise what he sees,
He cannot recognise peace though he would seize it if he could.

What is this place?
All is calm and all is bright
And everything is ten times the size it used to be.

And he sees a door, at least forty miles high, if not more.
Bang! Gunshot it opens,
He throws himself flat, back to his crater.

Rachel Koszerek (17)
Ecole Européenne, Luxembourg

LOVE'S THE ANSWER

We're all the same,
despite our cultures.
So come forward,
forget the colours.

We're all the same colour
when you turn out the light,
that's all that counts,
so let's not fight.

You don't have to look
like a beauty queen.
You don't have to be
like him or me.

We're all individuals,
but we've got one link,
that link is love
that will not sink.

Kristina Ward (11)
Ecole Européenne, Luxembourg

AUTUMN

The autumn wind blows
And the autumn trees sway.
Brown leaves turn weak
And fade away.

The days grow colder,
The nights turn long,
I have a feeling
There is something wrong.

The sun is still shining
The birds are still singing,
Animals hibernate,
Ducks head south.

I love this new autumn,
It's going to be fun!

Felicity Taylor (11)
Ecole Européenne, Luxembourg

WHY DO WE KILL ANIMALS?

Why do we kill animals for our pleasure?
Chickens and birds without one feather,
Lions poached, so are tigers,
Rabbits used as lab experiments.

Matthew Swithinbank (10)
Ecole Européenne, Luxembourg

MY LITTLE CLOCK

Tick-tock, goes my clock,
All day long.
Tick-tock, goes my clock,
'Til the break of dawn.

When I wake up,
You are still here,
Ticking along
Next to my ear.

Tick-tock, goes my clock,
'Til the break of dawn.

Daphné Seale (11)
Ecole Européenne, Luxembourg

TEACHERS, CHILDREN, BABIES ETC.

Teachers: order, manners and big words.
Children: sins, disorder, lies.
Babies: drool, slobber and screams.
Aliens: green, spotty and long, hairy antennae
Cats: hairy, sleek and sharp claws.
Dogs: bark, fur and a man's best friend.
Jberedung: manners, disorder, slobber, spots, hairy and
                                    a man's best friend.

Harry Reid (11)
Ecole Européenne, Luxembourg

TERRORIST ATTACK ON THE WORLD TRADE CENTER

A pleasant day in New York,
Car horns tooting, people calling,
Just like a normal day.

Children go to school,
Their heavy schoolbags full,
Just as they always are.

I drive to work
In a great big car,
Just like I've always done.

I meet my friend called Michael,
Who is mainly known as Mick,
Just as he's always known.

We take the big lift up
And sit down at our desks,
Just like we always do.

Phones are ringing,
Mail's arriving,
Just like a normal day.

Suddenly, a horrific *boom!*
Reverberates around the room.

Walls collapsing,
Rubble falling,
People screaming, running, crawling.

When high above us people die,
Safely run out Mick and I.
Not a normal day.

Richard Mann (11)
Ecole Européenne, Luxembourg

THE BUTCHER'S KNIFE

Have you seen the butcher's knife?
It's very sharp and thin.
You'd know it if you saw it,
It's full of meaty sin.

Many different cows and pigs
Have seen the bloody knife,
Watching every murderous death,
Holding on to life.

The desperation in their eyes
As the knife is taken out,
They try to kick, but don't succeed,
Whack! Blood comes spurting out.

Julia Graham (10)
Ecole Européenne, Luxembourg

FIRE

Fire burns like a lighter,
Fire, warm like the sun,
Fire, always growing brighter.

Mark Comfort (11)
Ecole Européenne, Luxembourg

BASKETBALL

Basketball is a sport,
You play it on a special court.

You dribble the ball,
No matter if you're small,
But it's better if you're tall.

The aim is the basket,
Or you can pass it.

If you make a steal,
That's a big deal.

If you can decide the game,
You'll get no blame.

If the trainer shouts, 'Time out!'
You'd better not fool about.

We play as a team
And we all have a dream:

To go on a big trip
And win the championship.

William Jones (13)
Internationale Schule eV, Hamburg

A DAY NOT TO BE FORGOTTEN

As I look through my window
into a white, white sky,
I see cuddly white, woolly snowflakes
softly passing by.

This is the day that many people
have been looking forward to,
gathered at a sparkling fire
sharing wishes to come true.

It comes as a sudden white, white bird,
gently waving his wings,
celebration, peace and happiness
is what this beautiful white bird brings.

I know this world is not as peaceful
as it seems to be,
but deep in my heart I'm still thankful
that life was given to me.

Kristien Steenken (13)
Internationale Schule eV, Hamburg

ALL AT SEA

The sea, the sea, the sea, the sea,
it rolled and rolled and called to me,
come in, it said, come in.
Rumbling and howling destructively,
the sea took me on a journey.
The waves swelled and grew menacingly,
as if daring me to fall into its clutches.
Bobbing up and down helplessly,
I continued on my brave journey.
So fierce were the waves,
looking like drooling monsters,
spewing streaks of foam through the air.
Suddenly, the sea grew shallow and peaceful,
swaying gently against the cool breeze.
In the distance I saw land.
Goodbye!
I said to the sea.

Alice McBurney (12)
Internationale Schule eV, Hamburg

THE LITTLE RED ROSE

As the first snowflake
Touched the winter ground,
Burst a single red rose into bloom.

When touched, it felt like silk
And when seen, it seemed like velvet,
So beautiful was this rose.

As the rose swayed in the wind,
People stopped to stare and gape,
So beautiful was this rose.

This rose looked so charming
And yet indeed it was,
Oh! So beautiful was this rose.

The little red rose
Had grown to be proud,
But with pride comes fall.

When the snow began to melt
And the air began to warm,
Fluttered the last rose petal gently to the ground.

Mallika Goel (11)
Internationale Schule eV, Hamburg

THERE ONCE WAS A CITY

There once was a city
That ran amuck
Then all of a sudden
Chaos struck.

The structure was hit
With extreme power
And down came
The beautiful towers.

People were screaming
People were jumping
It has been a while,
But the city is still.

All in the city
People heard a loud bang
The people were coughing
In the air, the smoke did hang.

Logan Caster (12)
Internationale Schule eV, Hamburg

THE BOMB

There she is, sighing in her sleep,
Dark is the night, dark and deep,
She wasn't to know
What will happen real soon,
That this night will be the night of doom.

Something came falling
From high up in hell,
Coincidence, that over her village, it fell.
People were screaming at its sight,
It looked lie a very big, black kite.
They ran away, but she was in bed,
I must say, very luckily led,
That she woke up by a noisy sound,
Outside, terror is what she found.

Disaster's the only thing she saw,
But no one really saw her again.
Lost or dead, no one knows,
No one will forget this day when blood flows.

Laura Brawand (12)
Internationale Schule eV, Hamburg

AN ANGEL'S VOICE

A shadow falls upon the light
And stars begin to shine bright.
I look down to see birds fly,
Up above into the sky.

I am an angel
And I can fly,
But I am not free like the birds,
I am heaven's prisoner.

This may seem queer,
But yes, it's true.
An angel sleeps in cushions of clouds,
But cannot travel about.

This is the story of my life,
There is not more than this.
Enjoy the life on Earth
And make the best of it.

My immortal soul shall rest forever,
Not only on this paper,
But also on this Earth.
You never know, tomorrow I might be a star in the universe.

Tizia Grabner (13)
Internationale Schule eV, Hamburg

SKATE AND DESTROY . . . YOURSELF

Aryan made the quarter pipe,
Sune said, 'Hold on tight.'

He struggled and juggled
Until grip tape was smuggled.

Luki's board snapped,
Willy cheered and clapped.

Adi popped then hit his head,
Thijs slipped when he was dead.

He flipped and fell
And landed in hell.

Tom said, 'The perfect run.'
His mom said, 'No, he's done.'

Yuhei Masuda (13)
Internationale Schule eV, Hamburg

NOTHING, IS MORE

It's black,
I can't see.

Everything closes in,
Everything comes with me.

I enter human,
I leave, an atom.

More than Jupiter,
More than the sun

It's black,
A black hole.

Marc Christian-Diederichs (13)
Internationale Schule eV, Hamburg

THE AUTUMN OF TIME

I close my eyes,
and as if a magical spell
has been cast upon me . . .

I lie on an acre's carpet of leaves,
under the autumn sky.
Leaves gently falling down
around me.

The scattered cotton candy,
in the dark blue above,
glides through the autumn of time.

The whisper of winter around the corner,
gradually making its way through.

The harsh wind stinging my cheeks.
My cold, numb finger.

But everything else seems like a . . .
Miracle.

In the distance,
the rising sun lightens up the ground
around me.

Far away,
hardly visible but there,
carried by the beam of light,
angels
fly towards me.

They take my hand,
and together,
we fly through the sky,
through the autumn of time.

Yuki Kakigahara (13)
Internationale Schule eV, Hamburg

THE CANOEING DISASTER

When this fateful thing
Happened one day,
The family was crying
In the most dramatic way.

The story is about two brothers
Who decided to take to the water,
They should have taken the long route,
But both thought the best was the shorter.

The trip was for canoeing,
Since they both loved it so,
As did their dad,
Who also wanted to go.

Following its current downstream,
They were paddling away,
When one of them saw a waterfall,
In front, surrounded by spray.

They tried to paddle backwards,
But the current was too strong,
They both fell down the waterfall,
Falling slowly and screaming long.

So now you know the reason
Why on this fateful day,
The family was crying
In the most dramatic way.

Oliver Marriott (12)
Internationale Schule eV, Hamburg

THE NEW FIEND
September 11th 2001

We had not given our old traditions anything.
For centuries we did not pay respect,
It was never given a single regard,
The tradition of living in freedom in a world of peace.
Our hearts carried the same endless goal.
For years we fought aimlessly.

The helpless lives that were wasted were just ignored.
We could not speak to them, we could not look at them.
We could only squeeze the handles of weapons and destroy.
The dream of a world of peace had blown away with the wind.
The wind never returns to the same place
The wind took the dream and left hate.

But one day something happened.
Something changed hate to fear and anger.
Fire rained from the skies and many people died.
Now a new fiend stood in front of us,
A coward without a face.

That day, chaos became order,
Hate became friendship and death became life.
From now on we fight together, enemies became allies.
Once again we prepare for fight, battle, war,
Mighty machines were built, weapons were made, we stood united.
Our dream of peace and freedom was drained by the thunders of war.

That day when fire fell, I knew for sure
Life could never be as it was before,
For the new fiend stood at my door.

Carl-Johan Rydén (14)
Internationale Schule eV, Hamburg

A STORY UNTOLD

A story untold,
A song unsung,
A trace in history left undone.
No sooner started, than dropped and let,
Forgotten in time, a watershed.

Take risks in life, go your own way,
For every one thing there is a debt to pay.
No one person can end life,
Without experiencing the counter strike.
Dark the day, lone the night,
Silver pearl tears across the sky.

Predators of an unknown kind,
At dusk and dawn hunting you will find.
To be stalked or haunted by one of these,
Will bring you shuddering to your knees.

These demons and traps are everywhere,
Yet sometimes we are blind to see
What lies forgotten down beneath.
No person stands on their own feet,
For in the end, parting ways do meet.

A story untold,
A song unsung,
A trace in history left undone.
No sooner started, than dropped and left,
Forgotten in time, a watershed.

Jocelyn Chignell-Stapleton (12)
Internationale Schule eV, Hamburg

DRAGONS

This poem is about dragons
Dragons big and small
Dragons that are blue and red
Dragons short and tall.

This poem is about dragons
Dragons that breathe fire
Dragons that are fierce and tame
Dragons that change colour.

This poem is about dragons
Dragons that are scary
Dragons that fight knights
Dragons that have treasure.

This poem is about dragons
Dragons that steal princesses
Dragons that fly
Dragons that are mysterious.

This poem is about dragons
Dragons that are mythical
Dragons that can disappear
Dragons that scare you at night

This poem is about dragons
Dragons in story books
Dragons in myths and legends,
But do they really exist?

Claire Stainfield (11)
Internationale Schule eV, Hamburg

WE BELIEVE

Tragedy is at their feet,
Slowly, walk home and weep.
So suddenly, so painfully,
So still, but unbelievable.

The dust is there,
So still beware,
Another one may fall.
So tenderly, just wipe your tears,
For the tears won't stop it all.

Don't cry, don't weep,
After all, it won't change it.
Gently sit and glare
'Cause we all have to face it.

But we are all with you,
So don't despair
And do take care,
We are all with you.

You say emotionally we won't survive,
But we all know we are still alive
And we will come through,
Because we believe.

Vivianne Knierim (11)
Internationale Schule eV, Hamburg

THE BIG CIRCLE

The moon shines with a bright light,
The stars will take you on a flight tonight.

You'll fly away in outer space
And see the world with its other face.

You'll see how everything spins and turns
And how the heart, the center always burns.

It burns with flame, with passion, ardour.
It burns for life, life that begins in the core.

Then you'll want to run from the flames and hide,
But you won't, because the big circle has one side.

It's the circle that we live in, it's the circle that controls us,
We want to resist, not to obey. But we must.

Can we fight that featureless, unknown power
That is in our little world every minute, every hour?

There is no beginning, there is no end,
Only the circle, space and time in blend.

The moon shines with a bright light.
You lost sight of your world that night.

Elena Tchotchanova (14)
ISSE, The Netherlands

ETERNITY

What do we know about dying?
Where will we go?
What will we feel?
And are the religions lying
When they say they know
Heaven and hell are real?

This summer was hard,
For I had to part
With two people I love.
Are they waiting 'above'?
Will they recognise me
When I join them in eternity?

Titus Trossel (13)
Morna International College, Ibiza

AIMLESS EXPECTATIONS

Look around you and tell me,
Is it real, what you see?
Warm welcomes, happy voices,
Smiling faces, not many choices.
Trapped in a net of social life,
Family tradition, fight with a knife.
I'm a girl in a world where the past quickly ceases,
It continues to crumble, try to pick up the pieces.
Surrounded by society full of contradiction,
Live with conception, afraid of distraction.
Not willing to fulfil the aimless expectations
Of a world filled with compensating deformations,
I ask myself who I used to be and what it was that changed me,
But time keeps running and all I'm left with are memories of
                                                    my history.
I'm only a girl in a world, pleading it to be comprehensive,
Afraid to fail, afraid of the world being defensive.
Suffocating under the net of total control,
Answer me a question; how are we supposed to grow?

Anna Bottcher (15)
Morna International College, Ibiza

THE MAGIC COAST

Sitting on the warm sand
I see speed boats that go
As quick as light;
Little girls shouting in the cool water,
Little boys making sandcastles and
Fish dancing in the waves.

After a while, a wave drags
A rock to the seashore
And destroys the sandcastle;
The children, sad, begin to cry.

The girls have a good time
Playing with bats and balls,
While the boys play football.
I hear the horn from the ferry
That starts to leave.

I smell the aroma coming
From the sea,
I see the pink coral enveloped
In green seaweed.
I see crabs taking to their territory,
Sponges and starfish.
When I hear the salt water
Crashing against the humid sand
Of the seashore,
It's like a chain crashing on the sand,
While the water recedes,
Leaving a line of bubbles.

The water is so crystalline
That I can see fish going through
The smooth pebbles,
I can feel water splashing my feet.
I can hear the echo of seagulls
In the gigantic caves.

The beach is picturesque
And free from pollution.
The majestic sea is mysterious
And full of different species.

Olivia Mari Royds (14)
Morna International College, Ibiza

DREAMS

Dreams are our thoughts,
Thoughts we don't want others to know.
Some we hold on to,
Others we have to let go.
Many times they are good,
On occasion, they are bad,
But never can your dream
Be like one someone else has had,
For your dream is unique,
Unlike any others known.
Your dreams tell others about you
And the secret seeds you have sown.
Your thoughts are buried deep,
Way in the back of your mind,
Unheard and untouched,
Unaffected and blind.
All are unrealistic
Smoking high on your mind,
Without the test of sobriety,
But in the midst of it all,
Your drunken dreams take control.
They reflect an image from your mind
Down to your drunken soul.

Jannine Helbing (14)
Morna International College, Ibiza

OLD MAN

There was an old man
Who lived in our town,
As I grew up,
He grew down.

Until he became
So crooked and small,
There was nothing left
Of him at all.

He shuffled along,
Eyes fixed on the street,
Only inches between
His head and his feet.

When for the last time,
The town saw him alive,
I had grown to a giant
Of four foot five.

And he was a dwarf
With a wobbling head
And a faraway voice,
But now he's dead.

Did they straighten him out
When he came to die,
To fit his small coffin
And where he will lie?

Beneath a tall tree,
Right under the ground
And as a hunchback as him,
His little green mound.

Rachel Kirk (15)
Morna International College, Ibiza

FREE-LESS

I realised I was committing my first offence
As I used my shaking, icy hands
To open the giant outer fence.
Now running and panting on unknown lands
Running, running, into the darkness
Powered by fright and focused by frost,
I kept on running into the hardness
Of reality; accepting, not knowing the cost
Freedom is what I lost.
But the questions still remain,
What will be the costs
Of this desperate act to regain
This 'being' I once lost?

Didi Trossel (15)
Morna International College, Ibiza

THE SPECIAL NIGHT

It seemed as though I couldn't find
The lovely picture in my mind,
But that was to the special night,
When you came in my sight.
I wanted to marry,
But you already carry
A ring.
In that special night,
I would fight
For you.
Why is
My wish only a
Fish . . ?

Robin Pieper (12)
Morna International College, Ibiza

IKARUS
A Dragon Night Flight

Shiny shadow, flashing wing,
sliding over brightness,
the glittering
massive body
with silver scale,
setting down
with a gliding sail.

Relaxing a minute
next to the lake,
licking the water,
no foresight to take.
Strains the muscles,
erecting the head.

The golden eye
stares through the night,
spreads the pinion,
ready to fly.
Thrusts off the ground,
it brandishes in the air.

Flies in the darkness,
up and high,
soars through the steam
near the sky.
Silver dragon,
but you're only a dream.

Anna Seitz (12)
Morna International College, Ibiza

THE DOOR TO FREEDOM

As the metal door opened in front of my face
and closed behind my back,
I slowly lope along the endless hallway
passing all my friends still behind bars
smiling at me wishing me luck
forty years of not seeing what the world
looks like outside this prison
not seeing the blue Mexican sea
not having those long walks along kilometers
of white beach. Only ice-cold snow
only grey walls surrounded by sad, unhealthy faces
as the colossal doors opened . . .
. . . free . . . at last.

Thara Bergen
Morna International College, Ibiza

VICTORY

Sprinting across an open field he could
Visualise the finishing line
Panting heavily, he had seen the trophy
That awaited him.
On and with one mile to go and no other
Runners in sight.
Roaring and cheering the crowd will be
As he breaks the ribbon that will set him free.
Trophy held high and spirit too,
With pride and honour,
He came through.

Stephen Kirk (13)
Morna International College, Ibiza

NOBODY IS TOO YOUNG TO LOVE

Love is an infinite melody
Of invisible notes
Love has its own flows
For even love crowns us
So shall he crucify us
Even as he ascends to our
Height and caresses our
Tenderest branches that
Quiver in the sun, so shall
He descend to our roots
And shake them in their
Dining to the earth.
Love has no other desire but
To fulfil itself
To be wounded by your own
Understanding of love
And to bleed willingly
And joyfully
Love is creation
Love is our life
Let's use it right!

Deva Allen (17)
Morna International College, Ibiza

DISTANT LOVE

Desire breaks my heart in two.
Crying is routine.
Feelings wash over me like waves,
Slowly making me drown.

I think about our last kiss,
Tears roll down my face.
Your eyes follow me everywhere,
But when I look around, you're not here.

Love songs are pure torture,
Silence hurts my ears.
I want to scream!
Emptiness, killing from the inside.

Torn apart by doubts and dreams,
Missing you makes me ill.
But if any love lasts forever,
Ours definitely will.

Lara Hunt (14)
Morna International College, Ibiza

POLICE

P   olice cars following robbers,
O   ver the hills they go,
L   oading their guns,
I   nteresting cat and mouse game.
C   alling help for the police.
E   liminating the thieves,

S   topping their cars,
T   aking their guns away,
A   rresting them.
T   elling them never to do that again.
I   nteresting clothes they wore.
O   peration Thunder is going on.
N   ever letting any thieves do anything bad.

Joel Kleinert (11)
Morna International College, Ibiza

CHRIST-MESS

Christmas is a time for joy,
(Hope I don't get a Barbie toy),
Jesus Christ was born in hay,
(I don't like them - you may).

People go to midnight mass,
(Hope they won't fall on ice - on their ass),
Singing carols in the snow,
(Throwing snowballs to and fro)
Decorating Christmas trees,
(Baking biscuits - yes *please!*)

Skating on the frozen lake,
(Getting so cold I start to shake),
Going inside for a hot tea and bath,
(Hot toddy and wine - I think I will pass).

Decorating the Christmas tree,
(Get it after, you'll get it for free)
Shiny baubles, candles bright,
(Hope they get my presents right!)
Brothers, sisters, all together,
(Hope they didn't ask Aunt Heather.)

Father Christmas down the chimney,
(Hope he doesn't hurt his thingummy - belly)
Presents on the good old rug,
(Hope Mum cleaned all the dog muck,)
Candles throwing golden light,
(Thank God, not a Barbie toy in sight.)

Turkey smells and mistletoe,
(What a great day. Ho, ho, ho.)
Tired children, fathers and mums,
(Me and my brother holding our tums).

All over for another year,
(They are making my presents, can't you hear?)
Father Christmas and his elves,
(I hope they look after themselves).

Felix Pau Soler (12)
Morna International College, Ibiza

THE GIFT

When I look at the blue sea, it calms me.
When I look at the sky, I feel its peace.
When I touch the water, I relax.
When I feel the wind, I get amazed.
When I see a cliff, I stop and think.

When I think how generous nature is,
I think how silly we are in destroying it.

Think how precious nature is.
We always think of nature as something really normal and simple,
But it's probably the most important thing we've ever had,
Without it we can't live.

I think we should give more importance to our *best gift*,
Nature.

Juan Martinez (13)
Morna International College, Ibiza

I AM . . .

I am a vegetarian lion,
Why can't I enjoy meat?
I am a crying hyena,
Why don't I have a sense of humour?
I am a barking kitten,
Why is everyone scared of me?
I am a roaring mouse,
Why doesn't the cat like me?
I am a flower, hungry for food,
Why do they just give me water?
I am a fast snail,
Why do I win all the races?
I am a car with feelings,
Why can't I go where I want?

Stanley Planer (13)
Morna International College, Ibiza

HORSES

Trotting in the fields
tapping on the stable door,
lying in the fields,

Galloping far out
as he flies over the jumps,
his white mane flowing.

Horse galloping,
his white tail swishing madly
in the hurling wind.

Maiko Dupont (11)
Morna International College, Ibiza

THE UNICORN

A massive stampede galloping over mountains
Suddenly coming to a stop.
In the sunset, a silver glow like a star above them
Attracted their attention.
A horn sticking out of a horse's head,
As white as snow and as sparkling as a diamond.
A Unicorn.
A Unicorn full of glamour, elegance and
A horn as pure as silver.
The mane with the strongest white on Earth and
Fur as soft as silk.
Fire, wind and water, these three elements
Were united in the Unicorn's eyes.

Jennifer Herzog (12)
Morna International College, Ibiza

COUNTRY OR TOWN?

In the town,
The grass is brown,
But in the country where we stay,
The grass is green every day.
The town is full of dirt that smells,
In the country cows have bells.
I would not like to live in town,
Because the traffic gets me down.
In the country the air is clean,
No traffic jams to be seen.

Nikolaus von Pueckler (11)
Morna International College, Ibiza

UNTITLED

deep down below
dangerous depths
of

agony
of

apathy

a baby was born . . .
             . . . quietly crying

for tender care
no care
will come

there's not
enough air
      to
         d
            i
               v
                  e
                      so
                      deep

falling asleep

dreams
are everything

when the tears
tear

never
fall away

stay

awake

Once again
I lie in vain
Once again
regret is my only gain
Once again
I'm about to go insane.

Magnus Brogie (17)
Norra Real, Sweden

COBRA

I am the eyes of the Devil
They glow like red-hot embers in dying fires.
I am what evil desires.

I am the emperor of the world's scorching sands,
They were moulded out of impure hands.

I am the song of an endless draught and venomous flood,
I am the master of killing,
For I leave no sign of blood.

I am the cause of silent pain,
Pain that never drains.

I am the slithering movement in deserts
Where no man can walk.
I am death entering a door without a knock.

I am master of dark arts,
So beware if you have a golden heart.

Shobana Venkat (12)
Rygaards Skole, Denmark

SCHOOL

When we go on a holiday
We have a nice long break,
But when we have to go back again,
There's something we have to make.

We have to make a project,
Or we have to study for a test,
And after a while you realise
You really need a rest.

You need to rest your hand
Or you have to rest your head,
And when the day is through,
You need to go to bed.

When you're feeling sleepy
And you start snoring,
You dream about the next day
And how it will be boring.

Oliver Miocic (12)
Rygaards Skole, Denmark

THE PYRAMID CHEOPS

Three famous pyramids,
All belonging to the same family,
Just different generations.
The father, the son and the grandson.

One, the biggest one,
Took twenty years to build.
It was a graveyard for the king Cheops
It was named after the king.

The pyramids,
One of the seven wonders of the world,
Have a mystery, still unsolved beyond it.
For it has still not been fully discovered.

Nadeen Elerkessousi (13)
Rygaards Skole, Denmark

THE DESERT'S SUN

Nothing in sight
Nothing to bite
I am so hungry
And above all thirsty.

I've lost my wife
And almost my life
Ran away to here
To escape my fear.

This desert is hot
Not a single pleasant spot
There is no place
To hide your face.

The boiling sun
Takes away fun
Heats you up
Until smooth feels rough.

My life shall end soon
Before the full moon
I feel grief,
But I must leave.

David Masek (12)
Rygaards Skole, Denmark

ZODIAC

Within all constellations,
Only your bright presence
Froze me
With admiration.
Your infinitely delicate beauty
Made me feel fortunate,
To have seen a vision,
Of your great divinity.
Your gifted smile
So mighty and powerful,
Like burning needles.
Suddenly
Your secrets
Started to collapse,
Your bright coloured burning patches
Emerged into bright red colours
Then to orange,
Resembling
A fire in a church.
Your brother came
At your dying flames,
With his fresh blue rays
To replace
Your brightness
With his dark colours.
. . . For you to sleep.

Vardan Azizian (12)
Rygaards Skole, Denmark

A USUAL DAY FOR ME

Today I woke up at eight,
My breakfast I ate,
I went to school by bus,
In front of me sitting, a big wuss!
I got a 'C' for art,
And in maths made a chart.
I ate my lunch:
Some pieces of 'crunch'.
Before I left school,
I did something really cool!
I won't tell you what I did,
It's a secret indeed!
But I can say, that at home,
I got really bored alone.
Before my mom and dad
Came home from work,
And my sister from 'Hork',
I was nearly dead!
The TV was on,
There would be a film starting soon,
About life on the moon,
How people there, hang on.
Time to go to bed,
What a day I had!
I now wish it was morning,
And the day was just starting!

Nune Nikogosian (12)
Rygaards Skole, Denmark

THE GOLDEN SPRING

The sun came in his golden suit
Behind a tree full of golden fruits
The birds singing in their golden coats
Beside a river rests a boat
Butterflies flying with beautiful wings
For they love the sunshine in spring
The sun shines into the farmer's house
The crow of the cock woke the mouse
The light wind blows
The white cloud flows
The goldfishes swimming in the silky lake
Followed by a hungry water snake
A child is walking along the river
Flash past by a car with a happy driver
Flowers were picked by a little child
Who is watching the horses running in the wild?
Fences were built along the road
Behind, is a pond full of stinky toads
The sun warmed where it is cold
The blue sky became the colour of gold
The sun sank down behind the hill
As the orange light reflects a shadow of an old mill.

Zejun Wang (11)
Rygaards Skole, Denmark

THE FERRARI

The shiny *red* coating on a strong engine.
The black smooth tyres on a sturdy pole.
The steering wheel with many controls.
The black leather seat waiting to be sat in
The accelerator ready to be pushed.

An all-time champ *Michael Schumacher*
Is getting ready for the race that may change his life.
Anything could go wrong,
Everything could go right.
The result is . . .
Ferrari, winners as always!

Caoimhe Ferguson (12)
Rygaards Skole, Denmark

THE NEXT STOP

Train ride home and the next stop's mine,
I've just got five minutes to get home on time.
I look at my watch and it's almost three-thirty,
Oh my gosh, I had better hurry!

Muddy shoes left by the door,
I switch on the TV and catch Channel 4.
What's this a new action movie?
Huge explosion! Whoa, this is groovy!

Rush hour and people colliding,
Camera zooms in on to buildings collapsing.
Shattering glass and twisted metal,
Chaos supreme and ending's fatal.

Phone rings and I run to answer it,
It's Mom asking 'Have you heard what's up?
Switch on the news, New York's been attacked,'
I look at the screen and it's just grey dust.

Stefan Liljeberg (12)
Rygaards Skole, Denmark

GUDEYBIHR

An ancient scroll of wisdom
Was found in the mountains near
About the wizard Gudeybihr
Who could neither see nor hear.

He lived inside a mountain
His cave was made of ice,
He had black cats and owlets
These 'pets' were fed on mice.

Just before the sunrise
He used to go outside,
And through his silver beard
He let his thin hand glide.

Then he would sing so loudly
His song woke half the world,
And then sighed even louder:
'This song I would've heard

If only just I was not
The wizard Gudeybihr
If only just I was not
The one who cannot hear.'

Then sadly he went wand'ring
O'er farms and fields and woods,
And then sighed very loudly
'If only see I could . . .

I would've seen the wonders
Of this exciting world -
If just I wasn't Gudeybihr!
If only see I could!'

Then he returned to the mountain
(If he could find it though:
With vision just like Gudeybihr's,
You can't see head nor toe!)

Ekaterina Shapiro (11)
Rygaards Skole, Denmark

THE EYE OF THE DRAGON

There is, in the eye of a dragon, the wisdom of an owl,
The brutality of an insane bear,
There is the cold arrogant evil of a snake.

There is the envy of a child,
The frenzied craze of a war cry.
The ecstasy of a toddler
There is the tear-provoking joy of a sailor returning home.

There is the grief of a widow.
The blind trust of a newly-wed couple.
There is the maniacal obsession of a gunman.
The never-satisfied greed of the prosperous.
The misunderstanding of man.

The eye of the dragon is like a looking glass.

Mikael Bjornsen (12)
Rygaards Skole, Denmark

HOMEWORK

Sometimes homework makes me sick,
Then I just want to kick it out
From all my life
And maybe kill it with a knife.

Sometimes I am happy about it
And want some more, a little bit.
Then I want to do it again
And again, again, again.

Sometimes I'm really bored
I can't sit on my chair anymore.
Then I go and read my book
Until I can't do any work.

Sometimes I'm so tired,
That I go to bed.
And I wake up when it's too late
To even start to do my work.

Then I'm angry and I'm mad
And finally, I'm really sad.
I think of all these angry faces
I think of all that mom will say.

In the morning, nice and shiny
                    When my eyes are very tiny
I sit in the classroom
And of course I do my homework.

Ugly letters I am writing,
Sentences have lost their sense
Just to finish faster, faster
All my life is a big mistake.

Ohh! At least I've done it!
I don't care what mark I get.

Ieva Pastore (11)
Rygaards Skole, Denmark

THE ALLEY CAT

It was a starless night when I first saw her,
The satin moon was covered by clouds white as snow.
Yet the weak silver rays managed to light a dusty path for me and there
I saw her.
She looked so elegant and comfortable in her sleek silver coat of fur,
This exquisite feline was silhouetted against the dark sky,
Yet her milky-white paw stood outlined against everything in the alley,
Her poise was refined and graceful, it was as if she knew someone was
watching her.
Slowly and elegantly she lifted her spotless white paw and began
to lick it,
I edged closer, she saw me but did not move.
Her silver crest was only lacking a golden crown,
And I wondered how this magnificent creature had come to live in
this simple alley.
Then the wind howled violently and scattered dead leaves all about,
And she drifted away with the grace of a silken butterfly never
to be seen again.
This phantom alley cat of mine.

Gergana Tuneva (15)
Rygaards Skole, Denmark

THIS IS WHAT AUTUMN BRINGS

As I walk amongst the deserted trees,
A swift, silent, chilling wind
Whips across my face,
And small crystals of sparkling snow
Land softly all around me,
Like sugar being sprinkled
Onto a bowl of breakfast cereal.
The bare, lonely and dark-barked trees
Stand out in contrast
Against the bright white landscape
Which lies beyond the forest.
The only sound to be heard
Is the rustling and crunching
Of the leaves around my feet
Being ploughed and parted
Like a tractor does to the earth in a field.
As I continue to trudge along
Through the old, withered leaves,
A solitary leaf is blown off a particularly gnarled tree
And lands gently into my hands.
I look down at the dead shrivelled leaf for a few moments,
Trying to imagine what it once looked like
With a smooth texture and a healthy green colour.
And I mutter to myself:
'This is what autumn brings.'

Tom Holm (11)
Rygaards Skole, Denmark

THE PLANET VOYAGE

I built a little spaceship
All blue and green and white,
I put it on my table,
Then I turned off the light.

I touched my little spaceship,
Imagined I'm on Mars.
I was driving through the surface
On one of my robotic cars.

Then suddenly, I'm on Pluto
It's very cold out there.
I'm freezing in my little spacesuit
(That's what astronauts wear).

A flash and I'm on Venus
How dreadfully hot it is!
I spilled a little water,
But it vanished with a hiss.

I jump around the moon
On the side that no one's seen.
No one would believe me
If I told them where I've been.

I flew back to Earth
And landed on a dome.
My first thought was -
'Home, sweet home!'

Gabriele Stakaityte (12)
Rygaards Skole, Denmark

A Pupil That's Great

A pupil that's great never comes late
And always does his homework.

A pupil that's great sucks up to a teacher
Until we want to throw-up.

A pupil that's great gets straight As
And never lies to you.

But let's face it, a pupil that's great
Is a pupil from outer space.

Ben Rosner (12)
Rygaards Skole, Denmark

Seal

Slippery seal all black and shiny
Eating fish all silvery, spiny.
Under the water you swim so fast
Unseen by us, until at last
Out of the waves you raise your head
It is time to find a rocky bed.

On to the rock with a clumsy struggle
I wonder why you take the trouble.
To bask in the sun, it is plain to see
You are after all, just like me.

Nina Scott (12)
Rygaards Skole, Denmark

PAINTING WITH WORDS

If only I could tell you how I feel.

The melon green grass, the bliss of chocolate,
The fat yellow drops of sunshine,
That slip down your back.
The sound of laughter, from the heart
Or a twinkle in the eye,
That makes you the matter.
The golden of silence, the fun of noise
The joy of people, or being alone.
How can I forget the music of rain,
The splendour of a smile
Or the kiss of the wind.

If only I can tell you how I feel,
If only. If only.

Kshiti Vaghela (15)
St George's School in Switzerland

THE SUN WORM AND THE DAYTIME HAWK

The sun worm and the daytime hawk,
Through the night and day, they'd stop and mock,
Till they'd say goodnight, but stay awake
And wait to sleep when the sun would break
And when it would they'd toss and turn,
You'd think one day that they would learn,
To work together like sun and fern,
One day they might succeed,
To heal instead of bleed,
The sun worm and the daytime hawk.

Philippe Bosshart (11)
St George's School in Switzerland

THE CITY

The city is a place,
Crowded and grey.
Full of stressed people,
Who have to go to work.
With cars blowing their horns,
On the gigantic rough roads.

There are people walking,
Some others are eating
In beautiful restaurants
With gold and silver walls.

There are skies
That are as blue as a deep sea
And trees that are as green
As a young free lizard.
And the air is playing
With hats, clouds and leaves.

Time goes fast in the city,
Like an enormous tiger,
Running, as fast as it can,
Through a jungle full of humans.

People chatter
About the Twin Towers,
The terrorism scares all the people.

The New Yorkers feel down
They think they will never get up.
They don't believe there is a God.

But once again they are very wrong,
For on their bills and coins
It says 'In God We Trust.'

Carla Gastelum (13)
St George's School in Switzerland

NATURE CALLS!

The bamboo tree whispered
'I've got enough flies to make me dull'
I looked up surprised
A bamboo stem cracked and fell on my head.

The skies called
'There's more acid in us . . .
We'll soon be vinegar'
I looked up scared
The skies went grey and poured down on me.

I walked through the rough
A strong wind rushed in
I looked up startled
The rustling leaves dropped all over my body.

Suddenly it was quiet
Fear overpowered my senses
Echoes of the sounds tore between my limbs
Like hot, prickly needles that stung my skin

Then, whoa! A chant
It droned on and on
From the mouth of the woods
Her voice repeating . . .

Oh *humans!*
How unkind thee!
Nature calls . . .
What you do will come back to you!

Anna Bernardo (14)
St George's School in Switzerland

A DEADLY ADDICTION

I gradually close my bloodshot red eyes
I fall deeper and deeper into the murky black tunnel of sorrow
I hear horrifying shrieks and loud screams
People are calling out 'Help me.'
But how can I help them when I can't even help myself?
I thought taking the drugs would make me feel better,
But it makes me feel worse
I open my eyes and the room spins round and round
Like a Ferris wheel at the fair
I try to call for help but the words never come out
My addiction to the drugs increases and my desire to live lessens
I feel gloomy, grey and helpless
Like a dying animal in the night
My willpower has died as well as the person that I used to be
I become weaker and weaker as each miserable day passes by
The drugs that I once took once a day is now an hourly habit
The smooth feeling pill in my hand stings as it enters my throat
I'm unwelcoming and unfriendly
I pushed all my loved ones away
When people come up to me all I see is evil fire-like eyes,
I pass out daily and often wake up not knowing where I am
I feel like crying and screaming 'Please help'
It's up to me to help myself,
My life is not worth living
I don't want to live
This horrible nightmare is too much for me
I close my eyes once more,
But this time I let go.

Shannon Hinton (14)
St George's School in Switzerland

A Moment In Time

A drop of rain falls to the ground
Although it splatters there is no sound
A ray of light shines through the trees
The heat's intense though no one sees.

A bird cries out for all to hear
While caterpillars crawl in fear
Below a dancing leaf drifts by
It swoops, it dives, it starts to fly.

The wind picks up and starts to sing
The trees join in and slowly swing
The clear blue lake begins to dance
While petals white like fairies prance.

Upon the shore a buzzing bee
His black and yellow warn all who see
About the air a scent of flowers
Turned to perfume by morning showers.

A trickling stream glistens slowly by
A deer bends down, decides to try
The taste is heaven she sips some more
An object blinds her from on the shore.

Cautiously she watches then nudges it a bit
Bored, she prances off away to find a place to sit
The small but shiny object's left behind upon the shore
On its face it shows to no one, that it's half past four.

Sara Bosshart (13)
St George's School in Switzerland

GENTLE, GIANT HAND

I miss the way you cradled me, deep within your arms,
A giant, soft palm reaching out gentle, but strong,
Embracing me to your bare, warm chest,
Hearing your heart beat softly.
As I sit and cry and weep,
I wonder if you hear me.

As night comes do you see dark?
Do you see the same starry sky?
I wonder if you wonder what I see through my eye?

I feel a deep emptiness without you here with me,
I wish for one more cuddle, or a soft, gentle kiss.
Are there angels there with you, or are you all alone?
I sit and wait for when they take me,
So I can sense once again,
The touch of your gentle, giant hand.

Megan Sahara Wood (13)
St George's School in Switzerland

FALLEN LOVE

How cruel can this fiend world be
To destroy that solid gold love from me?
For she was my single shooting star
Tragically lost to a speeding car.

We parted on terms of great anger,
Only for me to realise the torment I gave her;
Other faces see love as a simple game,
But how I wonder I'm not gone insane.

She came into my life straight from above,
When I lost all hope she showed me love;
The mourning of her has left me weak
That there are no words for me to speak.

My life a jigsaw puzzle torn all apart,
A punctured jet hole in the middle of my heart;
How she changed our world and showed great care,
No one in this world can ever compare.

Amit Patel (17)
St George's School in Switzerland

AND NO ONE WILL EVER KNOW

And no one will ever know how it is
How it is to be lonely, like an island in the middle of the sea
No one will ever ask me how I feel.

Everything is surrounded by people
They are everywhere
I walk down the street
I see faces, lots of faces
I am in the middle of the crowd but I am lonely.

And no one will ever know how it is
How it is to be lonely, like an island in the middle of the sea
No one will ever ask me how I feel.

I hope one day that no one will turn to be somebody
To be someone by my side,
To ask me how I feel,
To ask me if I am alright.

Ludmila Gutina (14)
St George's School in Switzerland

THE WATCHER

My life, unravelling, before the haunting eye
Which watches my every move,
Caught up in this realistic, nightmare,
Falling into this black hole, the abyss, of life,
As I walk through the valley, of the shadow of death
Why worry about the spiders in my head,
When there are snakes in the garden,
As the voices in my head swell, the whispers on the stairwell
Rise to a mind-blowing scream, telling me,
That suicide is always an option,
Tortured screams pierce my heart, already broken,
Cutting it in two, I am imprisoned, by my mind,
The skeleton of death, sucks on my bubbles of life,
Like fruit, from the Garden of Eden,
My hollow life, daunting, dark,
Glares at me, through the light,
I am drowning, drowning in life,
I want to shut it out.
The children's laughter rips at me, tearing at me,
Through the cold, harsh wind,
The eye, watches me,
It feels like a knife, cold and hard,
Eager to inflict pain, to kill,
My mind is hot like the middle of a fire, burning me,
Blackness swirls around me, no light can get through.
My life, bleeds for freedom,
The deep red blood pours from me,
Unseen by the naked eye,
Only the eye, the watcher can see,
They were right.

Suicide is always an option,
I shut them out, the world,
Shut them out, like an extinguished flame
My life, a door slamming.

Serena Cutter (14)
St George's School in Switzerland

MIASMA

A chill, icy breeze howls,
Tendrils of the thickest fog entwine
The shattered, drifting planks,
No lighthouse, no warning, no hope.

The screaming of my mind is dimm'd now
By the calming, bubbling, sloshing of waves.
The iron chains sink fast, yet slow
Far are the interminable depths.
Must I sink too to oblivion?
Yet life has n'er seen such clarity
And I am no longer
Enslaved, spiralling through the cool velvet blue.

Blue, vast blue the heavens sparkle
Shattering the thickset mist.
Gay, shrill laughter dances through the orange blossoms
Like light, I had not seen the like of so far north.

Angela Hitchens (16)
St George's School in Switzerland

WORLD'S MORNING RELAY

When the French young boy
Is talking in his sleep,
The New York girl
Is rushing for her bus.

When the Russian baby
Is dreaming about the giraffe
The Mexican kid
Is winking at the rising sun.

When the Swiss old man
Is tossing in his bed,
The Indian girl
Is still half asleep.

We are doing a relay,
From country to country.

Somewhere far,
Someone is snoring,
Somewhere far,
The alarm is ringing.

Minami Nakama (12)
St George's School in Switzerland

NOWHERE ZONE

Where nothing exists, nothing grows,
Where nobody thinks and anything goes,
Where time and space freely flow,
It's the nowhere zone.

Where you get confused just looking around,
Where you see a tree fall and don't hear a sound,
Where the secrets of the world are finally found,
It's the nowhere zone.

When you try to find and explain,
Your mind will not stand to contain,
In fact, you'll go insane,
In the nowhere zone.

Michael Foster (11)
St George's School in Switzerland

LIFE IS AS A PAINTING

Life is as a painting,
It can be beautiful and imaginative,
Or it can be depressing and empty,
Life is as a painting,
So paint well my friend.

Words are as colours,
They can be bright and powerful,
Or they can be dull and meaningless,
Words are as colours,
So match them well.

Feelings are the paintbrush,
They can be soft and loving,
Or they can harsh and cruel,
Feelings are the paintbrush,
So paint as you feel.

Actions are the inspiration,
Through them can be shown kindness,
But also there can be shown evil,
Actions are the inspiration,
So act on what you believe.

Christina Stead (14)
St George's School in Switzerland

ONE BY ONE

One by one
I see the drops
Falling just like
My life has fallen
And keeps falling
Until today.

One by one
The drops splash back
From the metal bars that
Block them from my freedom
Just like my life is
Being caged now.

One by one
The drops disappear
Glistening into the ground
Just like my life will
Finish in the end.

One by one
The drops fade away
On the floor and
Not even noticed
Just like my
Life which will
End and never
Be remembered again.

Faisal Akermann (14)
St George's School in Switzerland

TWO WORLDS

Tiger orange sunsets
Covered the sky with fire
The waves beat the rocks
The seagulls swam
Through the claret red pool
Of infinite mysteries
Onto the stormy life
Beyond the surface
Where the waves beat
Unrelentingly
And swallowed the unknowing
Boats and travellers
Down to the depths below.

These gloomy thoughts
Washed out with the tide
Left alone
On the shore were the lovers
Chattering peacefully, caringly
In the slight breeze
That swept all their worries away
A world of desire
Had been born
The ring was shown,
Happiness glowed.

Stephanie Hitchens (12)
St George's School in Switzerland

SOLITUDE

Closer,
Come closer,
I will not bite.

Can you not see,
That I am drowning?
Drowning in solitude.
My world is spinning in a mix of colours,
Scarlet, crimson, indigo, aqua
And in the middle me.
The grey in this terrible mix.

People see me,
They ignore me,
I am the odd one out.
I do not fit in.
Me the grey in this terrible mix.

They flick their rubbers at me,
They spit at me,
They scream at me.
They hit me with their rulers,
When the teacher is not looking.

They laugh at me!

I want to cry out,
Cry out for mercy.

But they continue,
Oblivious to the fact,
That all I ever wanted,
Was to fit in.

To be part of something!

Sebastian Montero (15)
St George's School in Switzerland

VELVET

Over the tunnel there was the silent ocean
Long, long ago, you told me
That you were looking for it.

The aurora was a picture, he said,
My home was in the deep cosy ruin
Where I could still feel the shadow of my father.

I stood in my empty armour
Feeling the cold bolt on my door.
I walk to get closer, he said,
But you walk to get further.
I screamed, but I was deaf
Then he was gone.

I was lonely again, but this time felt none.
But the seven folded dust of my soul
Was secretly forming a knife from my crystalline silent tears.

I received an e-mail on the violet misty morning
The bright blind white, slashed through my pounding dreams
Which were veiled with fears since our vale.

I'm walking, to get closer.
Sunshine yellow tickled my eyes
And I could not help smiling, in the azure winds.

Mayu Akashi (16)
St George's School in Switzerland

HOPEFUL DESTINY

When going up the road of life
I will come across hostile obstacles
And unbeatable foes
Wishing to impede me succeeding.

Walking on an unfriendly path
Hearing the sound of raindrops
Breaking the unbearable silence
I suddenly feel a disturbing presence
Staring at me with an omniscient eye.

I shall just hope for the best
Because I will be on my way.

Walking on the road of fortune
Feeling the cold wind
I will meet the eye of faith
Which would help me up the path of achievement.

Trapped in the blue ocean
Lacking of oxygen
I would just have to keep on swimming.

One day, what I left as a storm
Will turn out to be a cloudless sky
With a burning sun, welcoming my glance across the horizon,
Feeling the blaze of glory.

Catherine Kail (17)
St George's School in Switzerland

ESSENTIAL SENSES

If you could see through my eyes,
You would see what you look like to me.
If you could smell through my nose,
You would smell what your fragrance is to me.
If you could feel through my fingers,
You would feel what your touch was to me.
If you could hear through my ears,
You would hear what you sound like to me.
If you could taste through my mouth,
You would taste what your flavour was to me.

And if you could beat my heart beats,
You would sense your absence suffocating me.

Nidhi Chatlani (18)
St George's School in Switzerland

TEDDY BEAR

What would I give for a hint of a smile?
What would I give for a hug, so fragile?

Patches and stitches galore,
Unable to move, to walk through the door.

Fluffy and cosy when held in the cold,
Makes any grandparent return from the old.

What would I give for some light in your stare,
My dear, dear teddy bear.

Carla Pablos-Romera (18)
St Peter's School, Barcelona

TWIN TOWERS

The Towers fell,
Aeroplanes came,
People cried,
People lost their families.

People are desperate,
Lots of people are lost,
Are probably dead,
Thousands of people worked there,
That now are dead.

A war has begun,
Just for the fault,
Of one man,
That is Osama Bin Laden.

Thousands of people will die in the war,
Nobody would like it to take very long.

The Towers fell,
Aeroplanes came,
People cried,
People lost their families.

Silvia Jiménez (10)
St Peter's School, Barcelona

ARE YOU?

My heart is open,
open to you.
My lips are waiting
for a kiss from you.

Love is here again,
to make me feel
happiness and pain,
don't let my heart seal.

Have you ever fallen in love?
I have fallen right now,
I'm in love with you,
you can't imagine how.

Are you coming with me
through this path of passion?
Are you willing to love me
with desire and temptation?

Anna Domingo Miró (16)
St Peter's School, Barcelona

A TREASURE IN THE SAND . . .

A man travelling through the deserts, through the sand,
with nothing more but a rucksack on his back and a map in his hand.
He crosses half the nation determined to find
that wonderful thing that he always had in mind . . .
The graves of Collanthus and his wife Aset,
two great gods who no mortal has ever met . . .
One day, he finds a golden spoon, which gave him great pleasure,
on the spoon hieroglyphics were written which said:
'Mortal, find my golden partner, with us you will find your treasure,
let's see if this time you can recover what you want to get . . .'
The man went on searching for days, until one afternoon,
he finally found the other golden spoon.
This one said;
'In front of you there are three hills,
a staircase in the second one leads you to gold and a monster who kills.'
A bit scared he went to the second one known as 'the death of men',
and months later the man was never found again.
A statue in the square town and a medal were his rewards,
for daring to go in search of two non-existing lords.

Laura Amesz (14)
St Peter's School, Barcelona

MY LITTLE RABBIT

My rabbit is nice,
Twice like the mice,
His colour is white
And it's bright.

Running through the nature,
He feels the grassy texture
He likes the carrots,
Likes the parrots.

He's got a black stripe
On his white back,
His ears are black
Like his stripe.

He's got some sharp nails
And a little tail,
He is very sleepy,
But not very smelly.

He's got a little nose
Like his paws,
This is the best rabbit seen
In this world still to meet.

Florian Castet (11)
St Peter's School, Barcelona

I LOVE YOU

If you want to know,
How much I love you,
Look at the dark sky
And count,
How many twinkling stars
There are.

Count them from left to right,
Count them from top to bottom,
Count them in all directions
And if you think
There are a lot of stars,
I love you even more.

Meritxell Camprecios (14)
St Peter's School, Barcelona

GONE

There used to be two towers once,
where many people worked.
But now there's nothing - just a gap
the sky is grey, the day is dull.
Buildings destroyed as if a tornado had passed.
People sadly keeping away from that place,
no green trees just grey dust,
blood on the floor, people crying.
Cars which have been smashed,
by huge rocks that fell from the towers.
Firemen dying to help people from the ruins,
families that have been destroyed,
their loved ones are gone.
Why do we always fight?
It seems we'll never stop.

Danny Martinez (12)
St Peter's School, Barcelona

UNTOUCHABLE FEELINGS

Do I love you?
I don't know,
What I feel,
Is difficult to show,
When you smile,
The sky just falls
And tumbles in the sea,
Of your eyes of coal.

Déborah Aguilera (13)
St Peter's School, Barcelona

COLOURLESS GROUND BREAKER

My heart is black and white,
No colour to be found.
I open up my eyes,
To never hear a sound.
I trip to make you laugh.
My heart breaks with the fall.
I turn my back towards you,
As you pin me to the wall.
I set myself on fire,
So you think I am the light,
I try to surprise you,
But my face gave you a fright.
Can this heart ever been seen?
Can it be shown to you?
Can I see soft landings
As my ground breaks in two?

Elena Groenenboom (15)
The Inter-Community School, Zurich

THE MIDSUMMER FAIR

Little, wide-eyed, pretty elf,
Sitting there all by itself,
Sitting on a big gum tree,
Sipping at a cup of tea.
Others bustling here and there,
Tinsel glittering everywhere,
Lanterns swinging to and fro,
Making things look hundred pro.
Prizes hanging in small stalls,
Little elves shouting calls.
Excited tension in the air,
Before the midsummer fair.
Bugs hovering along,
Starting up a little song.
Creatures waiting for the call,
For the door that will then fall.
All are pushing to be first,
Ignoring the gigantic thirst.
Listen! Now the bells do ring,
In come wandering the King.
All the creatures start to bow,
Far away moos a cow,
The call is cried,
The door is pried,
Now the fairgrounds are wide open
And one elf gets quite soaken,
Beer is passed out, games are played
And little bets are quickly laid.
All rejoice in this great tiding,
For now they're allowed out of hiding.

Claudia Horak (14)
The Inter-Community School, Zurich

MY IMAGINARY RAINFOREST

If you think about the colours in a rainforest,
You mostly think about green.
But if you don't know about all the wonders,
There are lots of colours that you have not seen.

There are yellow monkeys hanging from trees,
There are little green dogs
And red medium sized bees,
But have you ever heard of pink and black frogs?
Or these little blue things that look like bugs?

In my rainforest that's colourful,
There are changes with the light.
In the day it's dark so be careful
And the sun goes up in the night.

Now I hope you liked my imaginary rainforest
And will come back soon,
Or else I don't think you're the best
And I'll shoot you up the moon!

Estelle Schnyder (11)
The Inter-Community School, Zurich

THE FIELD

It was so quiet while I was sitting in the field,
It was so quiet that I could hear my own heartbeat.
While I'm in the field, a rabbit goes by so peaceful and quiet.
If only the world could be so peaceful and quiet like that,
I thought to myself,
If only.

Carley O'Brien (12)
The Inter-Community School, Zurich

HALLOWE'EN

Hallowe'en may give some people a fright,
Because it is such a scary night,
Some people just like the day for candy,
But Hallowe'en is not that dandy.

Pumpkins, costumes, trick or treat,
Children all around the street,
Ghosts, witches and Frankenstein too,
All add in the Hallowe'en brew.

There also comes a full moon,
But it comes way too soon,
Then when it came,
Things would never ever be the same.

And then you suddenly remember,
That when the clock strikes twelve, it is November!

Stephanie Condne (11)
The Inter-Community School, Zurich

THE SHADOW

The shadow
It lays under us,
It guards us,
But it does not help us.
Why can't it be so?
Why is our shadow so black
and so dark and mysterious?
And then it disappears like
the light from a burning candle
gets blown out.
If there is light, there is dark.

Christian Boëthius (15)
The Inter-Community School, Zurich

EMPTINESS

When your fears are closing up on you,
When the darkness has captured you.
When you are running down an endless road.
Imagine me and I'll be there.
When your life feels useless, when there is no more hope to live for.
Let me be, be the one for you.
When all your happiness has run out,
When all you can do is sit down and cry.
Think of me and I'll be there to make you shine.
When your life is low, when there is no joy.
Just picture my smile and smile with me.
When your feelings have disappeared,
When you can't feel the hand touching your cheek.
Let me be the one to touch you soft and touch you deep.
So when you are surrounded by your own lies and your life is gone.
When you can't get up, when you are pushing
Yourself back down again.
When you try so hard it makes you cry.
When there is no light, no use nor hope for you.
When there is neither happiness, nor a smile on your beautiful face.
When you have neither joy nor feelings.
When your life has run out, when you feel empty and lonely.
Let me be the one to fulfil all you've lost and bring you back to life.
Let me be the one whom is loved by you and whom loves you back.

Nina Paitula (15)
The Inter-Community School, Zurich

MY LOCAL SWIMMING POOL

I like my local swimming pool
When my friends are there, it's oh so cool.
In summer, we can use the slide,
In winter, we must be inside,

It's cool and clean and fun to play,
I'd gladly go there any day,
We jump, we dive, we splash, we scream,
In your free time, it's just a dream!

Helen Clerey (11)
The Inter-Community School, Zurich

DON'T MAKE ME WRITE A POEM I'M NEARLY A TEENAGER

What are my rights?
I have no words to write down!

What is fair?
That everybody in 6th grade gets cheated?

I don't . . . ahh, it's difficult to . . . sort of ahh . . . you know it's
difficult . . .
always to be doin' . . . err the things they like tell you to do . . .
I mean . . .
don't get me wrong, it's just that I just don't feel like writing a
poem right now, tonight . . . actually any time . . . and I don't you
know . . . ahh! I don't even care ye know I mean if it's not . . . well you
know . . . good.

If I care will I despair?
Sitting for hours on this dumb chair.

When I get to school, I'll feel bad that I didn't do it!

Elia Brunt (11)
The Inter-Community School, Zurich

THE STEEPLECHASE

I pull up the filly to the starting line,
Her hooves are all polished, her coat does shine.
She nickers to me as I sit on her back,
My saddle is shiny, clean is the tack.
The opponents are ready, steeds pawing the ground,
The sky is clear, not a cloud to be found.
Bang! Goes the gun and off we go,
The horse next to us had a start that's too slow.
We gallop as one, my heart beating fast,
We're in the lead, not a horse goes past.
I count the strides, they go one, two, three,
Up in the distance, the first jump I see.
As we approach it, my horse is prepared,
We leap in the air, her courage is shared,
With the fans all cheering her loudly ahead,
Losing the race is the thing that they dread.
Her hooves touch the ground and we're speeding forth,
Oh no! She is heading far too far north.
We soar over hedges, again and again,
I grip her mane, her stride should be ten,
I count, it's seven, I hope we don't fall,
But she jumps too early and the fans do call.
My heart's in my throat but we do it just fine,
We soar across the finishing line.
Her head nudges mine, reporters crowd round,
My emotions take over, I hear no sound.
I knew she could win this incredible race,
So there was no surprise when she won first place.
Her big brown eyes into mine did stare,
And she knew that I thought we'd been a good pair.

Sarah Shields (12)
The Inter-Community School, Zurich

A PERFECT GIFT

Searching far and wide
Going black and blue
Trying to find a perfect gift
To give to you.

I thought of a necklace
The idea seemed quite fine
And to add a bit of class
A bottle of white wine.

How about something elegant
Like a diamond ring?
That would be so beautiful
It would make you sing.

Or maybe a dress
Made of satin or silk?
Of a white so rich
Exactly like milk.

Could it have been a shoe?
That made Cinderella a princess
Finding the perfect birthday gift
Is giving me a lot of stress.

But there came a bird
And whispered something to me
Suddenly my fears were over
As my worries were history.

The bird told me nothing,
But exactly what to do
He told me to write this poem
And hand it with love to you.

Zaosh Ghadiali (11)
The Inter-Community School, Zurich

HOLLY

My favourite dog Holly
Can be rather jolly.

If she's in a bad mood,
It's because she wants her food.

I take her for a walk,
Along a cliff of chalk.

And when she sees a river,
She swims and starts to shiver.

She likes to chase a rabbit,
Which is a bad habit.

Her enemy is the cat
Which is getting rather fat.

It makes me very sad,
When she's feeling bad.

She is my best friend,
I hope this will never end.

Natalie Greenland (11)
The Inter-Community School, Zurich

FRIENDS AND FLOWERS

Friends are like flowers,
They are all different,
Their weaknesses and strengths,
Different in shape and size,
They all come from different places,
Some are stupid and some are wise,

They vary in colour,
But all of them are beautiful in a different way,
They both need water
And grow at different speeds,
It's nice to have flowers,
But friends you need.

Flo Widmer (11)
The Inter-Community School, Zurich

A FOOL'S HAVEN

Obsessive imitations of the perfect one to be
A flaw, but not
So well disguised
That no eye
Can ever see through
That no mind
Can ever perceive
A toast to the master of disguise
Who saves me now
And lust so much encouraged
Now shall take its place
How sweet thine lies
That softly stroke
Now charm me
Use me
Abuse me
Seduce me
Not ever had folly so bright become
And the thorn that pierced so lost its sting
And will I to wake from this cursed dream
Shall I my own enemy be.

Hannah Yap (15)
The Inter-Community School, Zurich

MY EXTRA ORDINARY WORLD POEM

In my world
Sofas would be made from Oreo cookies,
Snow would come as popcorn,
Tables would be made from chocolate,
Walls would be made from candid sugar
And painted with white cream.
Floors would be made from cheese,
Books from multicoloured fruit roll up.
Paper from yummy dried fluff
And glass from glass noodles.
Nobody would starve again
Because everything would grow again.
Gardens would be filled with flowers,
The flowers would be candy
And they would grow every season
So children could always be happy,
Now everything would be perfect
For me I suppose.

Gissu Naimi (12)
The Inter-Community School, Zurich

THE OTTER'S FRIEND MOLE

There was an otter named Jim,
Whose mother was called Kim,
They lived together in a stream named Natter,
They swam all day and swam all night,
Until the sky was blue and light.
The otters had a friend who was a mole,
They knew him by the name of Cole,
He was very old but looked very young
Because he had a lot of fun.

David Lawrence (12)
The Inter-Community School, Zurich

WHEN I WISH

Yesterday I saw a shooting star,
A silver moon,
A golden planet,
A brightly coloured sky,
All shining down as they reflect their spirits on Earth.
In such an elegant way,
Since it's time to go to sleep,
The shooting stars take away their flaming tails,
A couple of sparkling sunsets,
On the eternal universe.
When one day, maybe in a year,
Just after the sun rises high up in the air,
For the first or maybe last time ever,
Flowers will bloom on the moon.

Elsa Lamy (11)
The Inter-Community School, Zurich

WALKING DOWN THE STREET

One day my friends and I were walking down the street,
Something hard struck our feet.
It hurt us, a lot you know,
It almost broke our toes.
When my mum came to see if we were all right,
We asked her if she could,
Tell us what it might be,
Which was hurting us so surely.
She said it was that little brat kid playing a joke,
And he thought he'd give our toes a poke!

Alex King (11)
The Inter-Community School, Zurich

MY SIS

The person I look up to,
The true Amazing Grace!
Like a pearl that glows within an oyster,
Shining as brightly as her face.

Her appearance is like that of a swan,
Gliding across a lake,
She's glamorous from head to toe,
But won't you boys just give her a break?

When the velvet curtains suddenly rise
And the music begins to play
In a group she performs, shining towards the audience
She just simply takes my breath away!

She's like the single gold petal on a rose,
Whenever her and the ensemble are on stage.
She caresses the gift of performing,
Like a writer caresses a page.

When a dance teacher tells me,
To imagine a piece of string,
Pulling my head upright towards the sky
(If that's what imagining can bring).

I never feel it coming from my head,
Nor pulling me towards the sky.
It's travelling over the many miles between us,
To connect the hearts of my sister and I.

Vanessa Aurora Spiteri (11)
The Inter-Community School, Zurich

PWP

I've got a great pony called Shorty,
She is only six but can be quite naughty.
The first time I saw her last year,
Was in Richmond Park, England chasing young deer.

She measures 13 hands,
Which really is quite small,
Her best friend is Herman,
Who is very tall.

Shorty is brown,
With a white star on her frown,
She has a long tail,
Which goes down to her nail.

She spooks and she bucks when I ride her,
When a big truck drives up behind her,
With all my strength I have to hold on,
But then I realise that she's already gone.

Shorty is Irish and a great little jumper,
When we fly over fences, she feels like a bumper,
She has won many prizes in her little pony life,
Each time she does, I say, 'Give me high five!'

Since I have moved, I miss her so badly,
But I know Shorty is happy and eats Polo's gladly.
And now we call her PWP,
'Pony with potential' don't you see?

Tasslem Von Streng (11)
The Inter-Community School, Zurich

POEMS ARE SO HARD TO WRITE

English lesson, Tuesday morning
Said our teacher, whilst we were yawning
'Now listen here, you noisy lot
Your homework this time is not a lot.
A poem you will have to write,
And don't you groan or put up a fight.'

I blinked my eyes, I blinked them twice,
What would the poem be about? Mice?
It seemed to be quite a difficult task,
As I sat there, drinking from my flask.
I thought all day, I thought all night,
What might be a good topic, what might?
I made a list of rhyming words,
Such as reef and beef and birds and curds.
Yes! I had an idea, one I couldn't miss!
I pulled out some stationery, and wrote this . . .

English lesson, Tuesday morning,
Said our teacher, whilst we were yawning,
'Now listen here, you noisy lot,
Your homework this time is not a lot.
A poem you will have to write,
And don't you groan or put up a fight . . .'
Now hang on a minute, this isn't right!
Why is a poem so hard to write?
And so I carried on, in the spot of the light,
To do the last few lines, I had to write.

Nikita Khandelwal (11)
The Inter-Community School, Zurich

THE STORM

As the wind howls through the air,
The rain thunders down and the clouds are dark as coal.
Lightning flashes in the midnight sky and the animals run for cover.
Rabbits hide in their little, round holes
And bears run into their caves,
Hiding till the storm passes by.
People look outside their windows and see the rain pouring down.
They close their windows shut and bring the blinds down,
Waiting till the storm passes by.
It is now morning and the rain has stopped,
People run out for joy.
There has been no flood, but trees have fallen down.
The sun shines brightly in the morning sky and the clouds begin to part.
All the children, all the women, all the men
Are praying that there will never be a storm like that again.

Victoria Mayo (11)
The Inter-Community School, Zurich

HAPPINESS

Happy, happy, happier together
Happiness helps me when I'm sad
If you are happy, I'll be happy
So that we can share the happiness
Together, forever, so that everyone
In the world can be happy,
And if everyone in the world is happy,
Then no one will be sad, and if no one
Is sad then everyone will be happy.
And that is why happiness is very important
in our lives.

Louise Bäckström (11)
The Inter-Community School, Zurich

THE TWO CAT'S LIVES

A mother cat was pregnant and had three kittens, but she had to give two of her precious sons away. The third, her daughter stayed.
So on the second day they had to go because their owners didn't want them any more. Their mother in pain, slowly closed her eyes and said goodbye to her youngsters who were homesick and non-loved creatures.

The next day came and they woke up to a new world. It was miserable and the room was small. They looked around the walls which surrounded them, they felt like prisoners. They heard footsteps outside in the corridor and the only door opened. They were scared and they hid behind the door and looked to see what would happen. They saw an unknown thing, a lady, who came and gave them some food. She also brought them a toilet and a bed for the kittens and two bowls for them to eat out of.

After their breakfast they fell asleep in the corner of the room and they dreamed. They had flashbacks of their earlier lives. When they woke up they knew what was going on. Nobody really loved them, the new people who owned them now, just played and fed them. Then they thought about how their lives were now too serious and that their lives were gone. Their brothers also played and fell into a deep sleep and when they woke up they thought that they wouldn't live much longer without their mother. One of the brothers was in a lot of pain saying 'My stomach is sick, I'm dying.' Their owner didn't notice what was happening and the next day one of them died. Eventually the other kitten was given back to its mother.

John Mallinder (11)
The Inter-Community School, Zurich

SPIDERS, SPIDERS

Spiders, spiders they're everywhere,
They could even be in my hair!
Spiders, spiders in the night,
They always give me a tremendous fright!
Spiders, spiders are easy to find
Especially when they're trapped in my mind!
Spiders, spiders, they're not that vast,
But they can be extremely fast!
Spiders, spiders and creepy-crawlies,
Always end up in picture book stories!
Spiders, spiders, they're in my bed,
This is the nightmare I'll always dread,
Spiders, spiders, beware, beware!
Believe me, believe me you're in for a scare!

Lawrence Fsadni (11)
The Inter-Community School, Zurich

I LIKE ...

Cheeseburgers, French fries, Jello and toast
These are what I like the most.
Pasta, video games, candy rings
These are some of my favourite things
I like ...
Cheeseburgers, French fries, Jello and toast,
Candy, corn, apples, marshmallows, roasts,
Oranges, pineapples, pizza from the coast,
These are what I like the most!

Kevin Donnelly (11)
The Inter-Community School, Zurich

My Passion, BMX

BMX is my passion,
It's extreme, crazy and hardcore.
And every bruise or cut I get,
I love it even more.
I don't know why I like it so much,
Maybe it's the height.
Whilst catching air, my mind is free,
And it takes away the fright.
Whilst pulling a tailwhip to manual,
Or a 360 to Smith grind,
It's like I'm God or something
The feeling is one of a kind.
All of my worries, sorrows and pain,
Just disappear, go down the drain.
I don't expect you to believe this feeling,
I don't think you'll understand,
It's believing in who you are,
And knowing that you can.

Mark Vesprini (12)
The Inter-Community School, Zurich

A Pony Poem

A pony is a wonderful thing
it will carry you on its back.
But I tell you, never trust it
or it will steal your snack.
A pony is very hard to control
it has always something on its mind,
Especially when it plays hide-and-seek
it is very hard to find.

My pony, little Bud, he is very very cool,
but when he throws me in the mud
he says that I'm a fool.
But whatever people say, and
whatever people do,
He will always be my best friend,
believe it or not, but it's true.

Emelie Forsberg (11)
The Inter-Community School, Zurich

THE STARS

Whenever I look at the stars,
they dazzle me.
And I can clearly see
that they are something special.

Each night they're there
and when there are no clouds
they shine bright,
and are a wonderful sight.

They support the people,
that need coordination
and most of them are always
full of fascination.

The stars are like good friends,
always there and
no matter what,
they will always stay where they are.
Thank God everyone has at least one star.

Anna Abrell (13)
The Inter-Community School, Zurich

THE CRAZY COMPUTER

Once we had a computer,
It was very well used.
And sometimes it got tired
And it almost blew a fuse.
One day it went berserk
And it did not work,
So we sent it away
To a place far away,
That was the last day
Of our very nice computer.

It soon came back
And I stopped in my tracks.
I rubbed my eyes and said 'This can't be!'
I thought we sent it to Italy.
Now, now, this is not right,
Who put it on the last flight
From Italy to Miami?

Well I saw it there,
On the carpet in the den, I swear.
It had a tan and polka dot underwear!
And suddenly it dashed up the stairs.
On its bionic legs (with hairs)!
I tried to run after it,
But before I could think
It splattered me completely with ink.

It took a lot, now he's my friend,
But he never lets me win.
It drives me nearly round the bend.
I'm heading for the loony bin!

When your computer goes crazy,
And you send it away. Beware!
It might come back from Italy,
In polka dot underwear!

Nelson Harris (13)
The Inter-Community School, Zurich

OUR WORLD

Precious time
should not be wasted.

Everything around you
is calm and quiet.

Absorb
the beauty of nature.

Calm and free
nature is the best.

Environment
is clean and welcoming.

Future lies
in store and waiting.

Use
your time for nature.

Love
and respect our world.

Laura Fisher (13)
The Inter-Community School, Zurich

WHAT I THINK ABOUT DEATH

I always wanted to know what happens after you die!
I thought, maybe your soul would live in a different body,
which was just born,
Or maybe, you will be brought into heaven to live with all
the other dead people?
In heaven, you would be able to watch the people on Earth,
Or maybe you can watch a replay of your life?
Another thing I thought about was that you would maybe just stay on
Earth and walk around like other people, but to them you are invisible.
But when I just think of the dead as being in a black hole
and all you see is black (like when you close your eyes and it's dark),
I somehow get scared, even if I still have a long way to go.
It's also just scary thinking about death because you don't know,
you don't know what is going to happen to you afterwards.
That's why I also think you shouldn't be thinking about death
when you're still under 60 and not in danger of dying.
You should be thinking about life and your part in it.

Jed Reiff (13)
The Inter-Community School, Zurich

THE HOMEWORK MACHINE

The home machine, oh the homework machine
Most perfect mechanism that's ever been seen.
Just put your homework in, then drop in a dime,
Turn the switch on, and in ten seconds' time,
Your homework comes out, fast and clean as it can be.
Here it is - 'five plus nine?' and the answer is 'three'.
Three?
Oh me . . .
I guess it's not as perfekt
As I thought it would be.

Yves Biggoer (13)
The Inter-Community School, Zurich

LOST!

I'm lost in the dark, I'm lost in the light.
I'm lost in my mind because of problems
and feelings.
I'm lost when I look for things and when
I get a problem to solve.
Sometimes I get lost and everything starts
to spin and gets dizzy and dim.
I feel addicted to problems, I feel drawn to
bad things and bad feelings.
I don't know what to do, I'm just completely lost.
Sometimes when I feel sick I can't see, feel or
smell, I can't find myself around the house
or in school.
I feel lost all the time.

Malin Lundgren (11)
The Inter-Community School, Zurich

ANGELS

I know an angel
He has beautiful wings,
He knows when I travel
And he knows everything.
He flies in the sky
He is always in a bubble,
He doesn't let me cry
My angel is invisible.
He is sweet and nice and
One day you will get to know
Your angel when he will carry
You up to the clouds.
I love my angel.

Alexandra Lowell (13)
The Inter-Community School, Zurich

THE SEA

The sea is mysterious and far away
It's dark blue and scary and far away,
Underneath, in the deep where it's very cold
Live different creatures, even fish which are gold.
I've always wondered why the sea is so dark
Far, far away, where you can find a shark!
It's nice where it's shallow,
Where the sea is light blue.
I love swimming in light blue water,
But why? I have no clue.
As I splash in the waves in the transparent water,
I enjoy myself really, as I splash in the water.
The palm trees swing back and forth
To the west, to the east, to the south
And to the north.
Under the sea it's just great,
The sea is endless, you can't see the end.

Valentina Lipanov (13)
The Inter-Community School, Zurich

SKATING

Skating is a way to get rid of things.
For me it's a way to get rid of thoughts and worries.
Whenever I skate I'm in a world of my own.
I forget everything and sometimes it's better that way.
In my world I have no concerns
It's like a trance that I'm in
And when I wake up, I long to be
Back in that trance, where nothing worries me.

Raphael Brunner (13)
The Inter-Community School, Zurich

AN UNLUCKY DAY

Today in Science class
We were looking at some gas,
When someone accidentally
Broke the magnifying glass.

Our teacher Ms Darbouze,
Accepted no excuse.
She yelled in her big outside-voice,
And the rest of the class screamed 'Boos!'

The poor unfortunate kid,
Then fell on someone's squid.
(The squid was an experiment,
For an older twelfth grade kid.)

The poor kid's from Kentucky,
He still sucked on his 'Ducky',
But too bad for him, his day was bad
And the poor kid's name was: Unlucky.

Kirsty Chan (12)
The Inter-Community School, Zurich

ONE HAIKU

I wrote a poem
In the form of a Haiku
Because I had to.

Derek Ressler (14)
The Inter-Community School, Zurich

LOST!

You're happy, carefree,
Just out for a walk
To get away from your home
And all the usual talk.

When suddenly you realise
You haven't a clue where you are!
Did you come by that tree
Or over there by that car?

'Where is it?' You think,
'Where's the place where I came?
I thought I knew,
But now it all looks the same.'

Staring round the street
Looking for something familiar
You're just so unsure,
It all looks so similar.

You panic, you scream,
You dash around, wild.
You crash through the hedges
And howl like a child.

Then you find yourself home
You missed it in your rush
And your family's staring and pointing
All you can do is giggle and blush.

Nathalie Hopchet (13)
The Inter-Community School, Zurich

NIGHT

The room was silent
no light could be seen
black; alone with my fears.
Then a creeping, seeping light appeared
flooding my room with melted copper light.
Creaking, the door slowly opened
a figure was in the doorway,
heart racing, fear paralysing me.
It was holding an object.
Was it a gun?
Was the figure a murderer?
The figure appeared as my eyes
adjusted to the light,
It was only Dad - *phew!*
I wiped my brow of the droplets
of water, sweat.
Dad was taking the washing out,
he picked up the washing from
the floor and propped it to the top
of the washing tower in his hands.
He turned to the door
'Night!' He said
'Night!' I replied to him.
Once again the room was silent!'

Andrew Higgins (13)
The Inter-Community School, Zurich

LOOKING FOR A SCAPEGOAT

The 11th of September started off as a wonderful day,
The sun shining in the faint blue sky.
No one knew that this beauty would end in such dismay,
Three aeroplanes changed their own and the world's direction
And now thousands of innocent victims and rescuers lie
Forever beneath the wreckage.
Giving Islam such a terrible reputation!
Can you make a religion liable for such a tragedy?

Joël de Beer (13)
The Inter-Community School, Zurich

MY GRANDPA

He's a wrinkly man with an old kind face
Who often winks and smiles.
Although he's eighty-six he's still got his fire.
A bounding cheetah at times,
Or a cat who just likes to sleep.
He's no good with modern day objects,
They tend to bring him laughter.
Christmas is his favourite time
When we're altogether.
Singing and talking, it's really quite a scene,
But grandpa isn't always laughing,
Sometimes he's simply reading the newspaper
And saying 'People these days!'
I love my grandpa, he's simply the best!

Sophie Moore (11)
The International School of the Algarve

ME!

M oney man and
A pple eater
T rying harder all the time
H urrying to class
I nsect hater, so often
E vacuating the premises and going
U nderground.

B uying better gear and
A lways smiling
R unning wild
B ecoming smarter every day
E ating chicken
R ocking the world.

Mathieu Barber (11)
The International School of the Algarve

ME!

W oman lover
I n trouble, non-stop
L emon hater
L olly licker
I t's back on the couch
A great TV lover
M arking the world as I go along.

J umping everywhere
O n the sofa,
N uisance to the world.
E xcept for all my friends,
S imply irresistible, that's me!

William Jones (11)
The International School of the Algarve

MY DREAM

There is a robber in the basement
With a bag full of spelling mistakes,
He is holding a banana in his hand.
I'm scared.

I ran away to the car,
Where there is a lion that looks
like my teddy bear,
He roars,
His breath smells like pizza.

I'm scared and I run away again,
Into the bathroom,
I trip and fall
Into a chocolate bar with flies around the sides.

Robert Cardoso (12)
The International School of the Algarve

THE COIN

I can't speak, I can't breathe
All I can do is a mournful weep
I feel pain, a horrid pain.
A coin is stuck in my throat.
Will this be the last time . . .
The last time I see mum and dad and family?
The only option left for me, is to spit it out!

It is out! Now I am free!
This misery, but now it's out
I am ready to scream and shout.

Hannah McFadden (11)
The International School of the Algarve

MY SISTER SAM

She's groovy and cool
Bossy but kind and nice.
Yellow hair, very bright,
She likes her boyfriend
Who races for her, but
Wait a minute - so do I!

We rock the Nintendo here to there
Walk the dogs, we always care.
Maybe observant
Normal voice
Don't get me wrong, she's very nice.
She's funny
And she always cares!

Nicholas Bourne (11)
The International School of the Algarve

MY SISTER

My sister is as bossy as a mule!
She is very alert, like an alarm!
Sometimes my sister can be very unforgiving
My sister is very tough on me,
And very tall!
My sister is as cruel as the Devil,
She could be an angel
Maybe Lucifer!
Anyway, she is still
My big sister!

Pasqual Phillips Fellgiebel (11)
The International School of the Algarve

DEATH!

Dark in a dream
A girl as quick as a flash
Dogs as hungry as bears chasing her
Thrashing noises
Worst night
With ghosts
The ground as dry as dust
Weather awful
Thunder and lightning
Rats as strong as oxen
Can't stop
Must go on
Maniacs and wolves as thin as rakes
Everything gobbling each other up
In the middle of the woods
Horrible and embarrassing
A lightning struck a house
Shrieking cries
I'm as white as a sheet
Scared to death.

Sásquia Phillips Fellgiebel (13)
The International School of the Algarve

MY BROTHER

My brother is very tall and good at sport
He went to Lisbon to play football
I went there to watch him
And my old friend were there too.
They were also playing, but they were in a lower level.
My brother's team won
And there was a great party.

He is also a great fast runner
He sometimes did some cross country.
I am not sure where he came,
But I think he was good.
He is faster than my dog
And faster than my father.
Sometimes he runs from home to the beach.

Jorden Wondergem (11)
The International School of the Algarve

BUTTERFLY

I wish I were a butterfly
So I could fly wherever I want,
I could see Adam and Eve
Go over mountains and trees
And see all that is radiant.
I could see the suffering
Although there was nothing I could do to help,
I could fly into the Galaxy and see the world
From high above.
Spying on people I knew,
As I look below at the world,
`I see the little people moving around
Like a colony of ants.
the colours standing out as I look at this
Confusing view,
The lake, like a puddle, ready to be splashed
And I thank the Lord for giving me
Wings.

Georgie Helena Burns (13)
The International School of the Algarve

MY UNCLE

My Uncle Anthony
Has legs as hairy as a gorilla's
He is big and tall like a giant
And his feet are like a clown's.
His arms are very very strong
And he has a six pack of stomach muscles.
His brown hair is very short
And his whiskers are very sharp.
He has a lot of talent in skateboarding,
And is nearly a pro.
But he also loves basketball
And always plays it with us.
He has a nice personality
And really is very cool.
He has a good sense of humour.
Once he got both his elbows dislocated
And he always takes me skateboarding.
When he was my age, he looked just like me.
He always plays PlayStation
And he has absolutely loads of videos
About all sorts of stuff.
And he loves table tennis
And sometimes, when he is annoyed with his parents
He goes on a huge rampage in which he acts like
A wild bull.

Oliver Simâo (11)
The International School of the Algarve

MONEY

What is money needed for?
To buy things
To buy food
To buy clothes
Money makes the world go round.

You need money to live on
Without money we would get nowhere in life
You have to work to get money
A proper job and a good education.

Abby Townson (14)
The International School of the Algarve

MOON

A door
was
on the window
and
my bed is
close to the hall.
Cat is on the lamp . . .
I saw one car
it was sitting.
The tree
it was next to a house
and
the building is above the moon.
Big ball is behind the sun
shiny circle is
on the moor.
It has to be
on a lunar field . . .
. . . I don't know!

Dasha Filazafovich (13)
The International School of the Algarve

MY BROTHER

My brother Charles
He is quite bossy,
But when he wants to
He can be funny.
He is really wild,
But you can't blame him
'Cause he can be
A nice child.
He is a teen
That's why he's being
Annoying and cruel
And especially mean,
But I still like him
'Cause he is my brother.

Emmanuel Guillon (11)
The International School of the Algarve

ME!

R   easonable
O   ral working maniac
R   ecklessly
Y   owling around

H   eated hands
E   erily humble for a
N   ap
S   o bored
O   paque, anyway
N   evertheless there's nothing to lose in my life.
                        Enjoying myself.

Rory Waylon Henson (11)
The International School of the Algarve

MY BROTHER

My brother likes to play golf and
he likes to work in the restaurant.

He is 25 and he is a little
bit heavy and he is tall.

He looks cool when he spikes
his hair up.

He adores music and he
enjoys dancing.

He used to play tennis with me,
and I like to watch golf on TV
with him because it teaches
us something.

Tiago José Banges (11)
The International School of the Algarve

A WALK IN THE COUNTRYSIDE

Hear flaming birds
Yodelling trees and
Cobalt berries
Smelling frogs in
A pond, and a Boeing
In the sky.
Dogs on the streets
Staring at cats . . .
A Sunday evening!

Andreas Zabari (13)
The International School of the Algarve

THE SUN'S DAZZLING SPARKLE

In the mornings, day of sunrise
Where the sunlight dazzle starts
If I see its glittering glinter
I know the powerful day begins.

The heavenly skies look so light-hearted
Just like children in a whirl of giggling,
Everything is so cheery, so joyful and bright
It lets my dead spirit break free.

Now the day is gone and done,
Now that the sun's little sparkle has faded
There is only faint grim colours in the sky
It's joyless and senseless.

So all I do is pause till my destiny gets its turn again.

Stefanía Bjöginsdóttir (14)
The International School of the Algarve

ME!

I was really lucky
One day I was in the Intermarche when
I found 5000 escudos lying on the floor.

I picked it up and bought an Eminem CD with it.
My favourite books are Goosebumps,
They are very thrilling and scary
I have the whole set of the 2000 Goosebump books.
When I'm older I would like to be in the army
Because I would like to travel the world
And help people in need.

Robert George Parker (11)
The International School of the Algarve

ME!

Me!
When I
broke my arm,
in my old school
all I could feel was pain,
I had to go to hospital,
and I did, with my mum and dad.
They were worried, I didn't go to school
for two weeks, my mum had to stay at home,
my dad had to go to work.
When I got better, my
mum could go to
work and I
could go to
school.

Daniel Martins (11)
The International School of the Algarve

NEW YORK

Living in New York
where the Empire State Building stands,
above the dark, deep, misty sea . . .
Dreaming of a countryside
on the other side of the sea . . .
Where they have flying pigs
and cows which smell of cheese.

Joshua Muzaffer (13)
The International School of the Algarve

ME!

P   rogressing in maths
A   nt interest
T   ea lover
R   eally happy
I   mpressed with myself
C   at hater
K   ind person

H   awk admirer
A   lways smiling
W   arhammer 40000 fan
K   iwi lover
E   ater of chicken
R   ather unusual boy.

Patrick Hawker (11)
The International School of the Algarve

TRANQUIL DREAMS

It slithers and slips
Through earth-torn caverns,
Echoing through the depths of your subconscious.
Waves wash back and forth,
Sighing
In a mind of dreams and fantasy.
A thought,
So precious you can only whisper it
Or it might float away.
You wake,
In a sweaty sleep,
It all leaves your head.

Moira Nicolson (13)
The International School of the Algarve

GRANDPA

My grandpa is cool
He rides motorbikes and watches TV,
But sometimes he is a little grumpy
And that's not cool
He likes history and stuff,
But sometimes he is a little grumpy
And that's not cool.
He likes to build things and to write,
But sometimes he is a little grumpy
And that's not cool.
He is snoopy and wants to know everything.
But sometimes he is a little grumpy,
But most of the time he is
      Cool!

Sebastian Dyt (12)
The International School of the Algarve

INFINITE

Alone!
I am wondering what to say
Walking in the streets,
It's freezing
I hear noises everywhere.
The sky is grey
It starts to rain
I look at my hands
They are full with blood and cold
I see crowds of people walking by,
I am scared.
My conscience tells me to go home,
Then I do.

Charlotte Pader (13)
The International School of the Algarve

MY SISTER LINDSEY

Lindsey is very friendly
And appealing too
She is very creative
With her paintings and drawings.

Lindsey is wiry
As well as mild,
She's very considerate,
An attentive child.

Lindsey is harsh,
She's fifteen years old,
She is my sister
Or so I've been told.

I like talking to her
As a sister, as a friend,
I like going places with her
And I hope this won't end.

Alexandra McClary (11)
The International School of the Algarve

DREAMS

I walk down the path of life
And as I walk, I dream.

I dream of love and hate,
I laugh and cry and smile.

In my dream, I live
In my life, I dream

And as dreams become clear
And waking becomes dream

I know.

I know what path to choose
And that my choice is right -

I dreamed it once.

Hila Peer (15)
The International School of Brussels

'I RESPECT YOU'

'I respect you,'
said the novelist
to the poet.

'You say so
much in
such few words.

I wish I
were more
like you.

Trimming my
novels into
short poems.'

Said the poet
to the novelist,
'Your stories are
as beautiful as
my poems.'

Kim Smouter (18)
The International School of Brussels

BE ME A MOTHER . . .
(Inspired by Angelou's style in
For Us, Who Dare Not Dare)

Be me a mother
Provide me gorgeous children, healthy and strong
Find me the father, his wide loving arms to hold me
protective wings
sheltering me from the strong wind
of the dangerous, yet passionate storm.

Fly me wings
Soar me across the treacherous ocean that lies under me
dark blue horizons that search
for souls to drown.

Carry me children, through the phase of childhood itself
and welcome me adult
speak me principle
red and white hues of ribbon that grasp the diploma as it awaits
the palms of my hand.

Taste me success
its spices flavoured in accomplishment
drenching the tender meat of apprehension that comes
with teenage fear

Panic me, excite me, love me, unite me,

Independence.

Hilary Sweatt (16)
The International School of Brussels

THE CARIBBEAN

The Caribbean is a sunny beautiful region with fantastic islands,
The beaches are as nice as you dream.
The water is wonderful,
It is light blue, but with a lot of salt in it.
You can go scuba-diving
Which is great.
You see blue, yellow and red, all kinds of fish.
The coral is as sharp as knives.
Sharks swim around you, they ignore you,
But when you distract them
You get eaten up!

Christian Dahlskog (12)
The International School of Lausanne, Switzerland

THE NIGHT

The sun is going to sleep
The blue sky with grey clouds
Is getting dark and thick

The round and clear moon
Shines amongst the clouds
Whilst I'm lying on the bed
And closing my eyes soon

Dreams will come to me
And a new day with yellow sun
Will be ready to start and see.

Marta Frigolé Vivas (11)
The International School of Lausanne, Switzerland

I WANT TO SEE

I can smell
I can touch
I can feel
I can taste
Yet I can't see.

I want to know the colours of the beautiful flowers,
I want to see the splendid sun
gently setting over the horizon.

I want to look at the golden, yellow and brown
autumn leaves amongst us.
I want to see the ocean rippling against the shore.

I want to see the swift agile tiger,
I want to see the fresh white snow
glistening in the sun.
I want to see all the world's cultures and religions,
But most of all I want to see your face.

Julián Zbar (11)
The International School of Lausanne, Switzerland

THE MOON

On the moon your footsteps will stay
Because the wind won't blow them away,
No gravity, imagine how that would be.

If you ever go there, please tell me,
Because then I will keep you company.
No gravity, imagine how that would be.

As you float around, you don't make a
Single sound,
No gravity, imagine how that would be.

As you go back, you wish you could stay
Instead of coming back another day.
No gravity, imagine how that would be!

Ulrika Nilsson (11)
The International School of Lausanne, Switzerland

THE BLACK SLOPE

I look down at this giant hill filled with snow
Watching another skier
Suddenly he falls and slides down the mountain
I decide I do not want to go,
But I look back and see a hill almost as steep as the black one
And I think 'I'm not walking up that!'

I finally decide to try the black slope
I take great care in every move I make,
Trying not to skid and slide down the mountain.

Twenty to thirty minutes,
But I make it!
Victory!
Everyone cheers for me
Because I did it!
I have passed the test,
Which many people have failed.

Roxane Pietro (11)
The International School of Lausanne, Switzerland

THE A-BOMB

A weapon never even imagined,
A force of destruction so strong.
A detonator of fear
The Atom Bomb
The fear of all.
The one so powerful,
It will only gain more power.
The weapon of all time
A weapon that will never be overcome
Except by its own.
The Atom Bomb
The worst mistake
Yet.

Luke Hide (13)
The International School of Lausanne, Switzerland

AUTUMN IS HERE

Autumn is here
You can smell it in the air.
The leaves all change
To yellow, brown and red.
The lake is warm
The water is calm,
And people relax in the sun.
The dogs run free
In the grass.
Children play in the warm autumn breeze.
Summer has gone,
Autumn is here.

Jonathon Nursey (12)
The International School of Lausanne, Switzerland

I'M SORRY

I'm sorry I hit you
I'm sorry I said I hate you.
I'm sorry I kicked you.
I'm sorry I jumped on you,
I'm sorry I pushed you.
I'm sorry I destroyed your model.
Do you forgive me?
What! You don't! Well I'm not
Sorry I hit you, pushed you, kicked you.
Destroyed your model, jumped on you and
I still hate you.
What do you say to that?

I'm sorry *Big Brother!*

Timothy Williams (11)
The International School of Lausanne, Switzerland

SAILING

Sailing is the best thing you can do on sunny days,
The sailing boat goes up and down
On the bumpy waves,
You pull the rope
When the sail is fluttering
The boat goes faster and faster,
It is funnier if it is sunny.
If you capsize,
It is not a disaster,
It is always great fun.

Axel Bernhard-Larson (11)
The International School of Lausanne, Switzerland

THE DEATH OF A SINNER

The heat is intense
On the way down through the thin corridor
The imps are all around
Bugging me
Sending me on the long way down to insanity
Slowly and painfully.
My heart is filling up with hatred.

Suddenly . . .
The corridor is lit with a dark red light!
I get a small pinch of hope,
But it is only the fires of hell.

Pain bursts out in flames,
Stinging something chronic.
The itching brings me to the brink of insanity,
Everything brings back the long forgotten memories,
Memories of my sinful life.

After that the feeling of falling,
And the smack, crack and scream,
Of landing on my back.
The terrifying pain
Of landing in sizzling hot lava
And bubbling oil.
The horrifying screams pierce my ears,
As the frightened sinners beg for mercy.

Suddenly . . .
I wake up in my own room.
I silently give back the pennies
Which I stole from my sister last night.

Kalle Fredrikson (12)
The International School of Lausanne, Switzerland

Who Is This?

Who is this person who yells and screams?
Who is this person who gets all the attention, or so it seems?

Who is this person who gets the TV before I do?
Who is this person who hits me with my own shoe?

Who is this person who tears up my work from school?
Who is this person who breaks more than one rule?

Who is this person who draws on the floors?
Who is this person who goes into my drawers?

Who is this person who gets into mischief without a sound?
Who is this person who follows me around?

Who is this person who says 'Give me that!'
Who is this person who always gets this and that?

Who is this person who gets carried or strolled?
Who is this person who's not so old?

Who is this person who gives me so much pain?
Who is this person who is driving me insane?

Can you guess? Do you really want to know who?
She's my baby sister Cara, who is only two!

This destroyer, this mess-maker, this loud smelly thing,
She's my sister, I love her, I wouldn't trade her for anything!

Lon Nunley (11)
The International School of Lausanne, Switzerland

THINKING AHEAD

You never know what will happen next,
The future's ahead, far from now,
But there's one thing I know,
It's when I get old,
I'll have fun and not let life get me down,
No cares, no worries,
Not as good as my youth,
But I'll survive.
I'm gonna do as much as I can before I die,
No matter what it takes, I'll try.
I'll live in my life at the edge of a cliff,
Jumping from planes, plunging to the ground,
Climbing mountain peaks,
Till my body goes stiff,
So high I can see the whole world at my feet,
I'll dive to the bottom of the ocean,
Exploring the depths,
Where the pressure's so great I feel my head being crushed,
Not caring about the possibility that I may die,
I'll keep going till my bones are dust.
Visit all the places where I wanted to go,
Do all the things I wanted to do.
There'll be nothing to lose,
So I won't have to choose,
Between danger or safety,
Right or wrong,
I'll just go on.

Then when I get too old to have my fun,
I'll probably end up sitting in a bar,
Smoking a cigar,
With a friend by my side,
We'll talk about the past,
And wish it would last.

A boring end,
But all the same,
I would have had my life,
It's hard to face,
The end of the game.

Henry Whittaker (14)
The International School of Lausanne, Switzerland

THE HOLE

I am swinging on the swing
I hear the telephone ring
I jump up high in the air,
You can barely see me all the way up there.
I am coming down as fast as an aeroplane,
When I hit the ground, it's just not the same.
I have gone right through the pre-solid earth,
Will I land in China or maybe Perth?
I am falling so fast, I can't see around me,
I wish I was in my house, with my family.
So I keep falling down and down . . .
I hope there are pillows instead of the ground.
I look down. *Oh no!* I see rocks,
I try to make parachutes out of my socks.
The ground is coming closer
I am ready for that final smack.
I fall off my bed, right on my back.
I'm glad it was just a dream!

Alex Ingram (11)
The International School of Lausanne, Switzerland

THE SEA

The sea is a big wave of blue
Draped over land.
The sea looks like crystals
When the sun hits it.

When you dive into the clear blue water,
You feel its refreshing coolness.

When I am swimming
I feel I am the sea.
I am the sand, and the seaweed
I am the rocks, and the fishes,
I am the starfish.

The fishes dart here and there,
And I wonder what it would be like,
Living in the deep of the sea?

That I will never find out
Unless maybe in my next life.

Linnea Jonsson (12)
The International School of Lausanne, Switzerland

MY PEN

My pen stabs at assignments
Given by teachers who
Think I don't know anything
I just say 'Pooh, pooh!'

My pen is quite dirty
And very grubby too
Which is funny because
It cost five francs twenty-two!

Everyone's got fancy pens
Which take ages to work
Shake, splatter, shake, shake,
And they start with a jerk!

My pen's got me gold stars
And prizes for its rhymes
I'll eat myself if you can find
A better pen than mine.

Caroline Bottger (11)
The International School of Lausanne, Switzerland

WHEN I GET OLD

When I get old
Don't send me off to an Old Folk's Home.
I don't want to sit around all day
Remembering the fun times,
Which I used to enjoy.
I want to live them!
I want to go skydiving
Or bungee-jumping from
The Golden Gate Bridge.
I don't want to depend on people
I want people to depend on me!
I don't want to sit around a fire
Telling boring stories of the past
To a room of half-asleep ghosts.
I want to get together
With a group of groovy grannies
And have an all-night party!
Please, when I get old
Don't send me off to an Old Folk's Home,
To end my days in silence.

Jessica Leffert (14)
The International School of Lausanne, Switzerland

FRIENDSHIP

We will stay friends until the end of time
And I'd like to share your friendship
With other friends of mine

This I've learned
Through the years
That friendship is earned
Along with tears.

But nothing's holding us back
Now let's move on to a new track
From here to beyond.

Friends part,
But your friendship
Will always remain in your friend's heart.

Peder Gronvall (11)
The International School of Lausanne, Switzerland

A BEAUTY

She walks, her body as big as a boulder
And armoured with shimmering scales.
She talks, her deep raspy voice has
Only been heard by a daring few.
She has so much inner beauty,
But shuts it out from the rest of the world.
Most don't know her and some have never
Even seen her; yet the brave ones search long and wide.
She hides in a faraway forest, and there she lies with nothing but
Solitude. They observe her with extreme amounts of pointless hatred.
She is a treasure of infinite worth, with a calm serene soul.
She is the dragon.

Catalina Zbar (13)
The International School of Lausanne, Switzerland

NEW PLACES

The swaying leaves,
Red, yellow, green and orange.
Rustling in the breeze.
Drip, drop, drip, drop,
Trickles the water over the side of the shear cliff.
It becomes a stream,
Bending round boulders sweeping down onto the valleys,
It flows.

Suddenly rocky faces fill the cliffs,
Rough and jagged rocks,
Poke out around us like a pincushion.
I clambered into the complicated tunnels,
Dark damp,
Suddenly the light floods in,
We have reached the end.

Polly Robertson (14)
The International School of Lausanne, Switzerland

DEEP IN SPACE

Planets that go round and round,
There is no stopping, no out of bounds
Endless distances, light years away,
Stars I can see from where I lay.

Extraterrestrial like ET
Could come from Mars, Jupiter or maybe Mercury.
Space shuttles, spaceships, spacesuits and spacecrafts,
Used for people to shoot up into the stars.

NASA is planning to send people to Mars,
Rockets stand there, ready for take-off.

Steven Hiltermann (11)
The International School of Lausanne, Switzerland

THE FLY

You stop on my nose
Park on my head,
Rest on my shoulder
And when you move to my arm
I move my hand uselessly
To kill you,
But you take flight
And land on my pencil.
My pencil case and books
Still await your arrival.

People tell me that you could
Bring terrible harm,
But I don't believe them,
And wherever I go
I seem to run into you
Again and again
Bothering me with your buzzing
And surely only idiots
Buy fly swatters
To chase you
Until they fall and break a leg
And then leave you alone.

Henri Suominen (11)
The International School of Lausanne, Switzerland

TIME

Here I am walking one cold winter's night
Pondering if my time is near,
That time that people always fear
Asking myself
Will it happen in a month or a year?

Off in the distance I see a gentle light,
But it slowly disappears out of sight,
I feel as small as an elf as I walk by some colossal trees
I feel a gentle breeze as I fall to my knees
Knowing my time has come.

Adam Dean (13)
The International School of Lausanne, Switzerland

DON'T

When I grow old
Don't put me in a home and send me cookies,
Don't leave me there to play bingo
And count my friends who have passed away.
Just get me a Harley
And let me ride the open prairies.
Don't leave me chained to my armchair
Listening to old men talking
About the war they never fought.
If you do this, I will shoot myself
If you shut me up
With only old men for company
Without underwear and unshaven faces,
I will shoot myself.
I want to smoke weed and drink vodka,
Not sit in a nursing home
Drinking milk
While I look out of the window
At life racing by,
Longing for my youth to return.

Gustav Stuge (14)
The International School of Lausanne, Switzerland

FOOTSTEPS

Footsteps, footsteps
One after another.
We scurry around
One like the other.

We are always in a hurry
We move around.
It is like we are looking for something,
Which will never be found.

We get faster and faster,
Every step we take.
We never slow down
To take a break.

We are in a race,
Which nobody will win,
Until we throw our differences
In the bin.

Our feet ache,
But we don't care.
We must end the race,
Like the rabbit and the hare.

But still we run,
From our fears.
It is a disease,
That can't be cured over years.

Footsteps, footsteps,
One after another.
We scurry around,
One like the other.

Kristen McKnight (11)
The International School of Lausanne, Switzerland

FIRE

As a match falls to the ground
It starts
The grasses and trees
Catch on fire.
As the progressive
Lashing flames
Grow
And grow!
The deep red
Bright yellow and orange,
Black smoke!
The alarm is sent
All the animals start to panic
And run.
A stampede of dismayed creatures,
Everywhere!
The fire catches the slow ones,
And destroys everything in its passage!
Having no mercy!

Now the only thing left is a graveyard of dead,
Grass
Trees
Animals

It starts to rain,
Some grasses are still smoking,
A dead silence hangs around
The cries of animals in the flames
Flash back and forth
In you.

The sadness of the end.

Audrey Fahrny (11)
The International School of Lausanne, Switzerland

MY FAMILY

My family are a weird bunch,
There's Grandma Jean who is like a witch
She has pills and potions for every illness.
We can't forget good old Grandpa Alan
Who is the world's greatest car fanatic.

There're all those aunts and uncles,
And distant relatives, some I don't even know,
But they're still weird as well.

There're all my little cousins,
Now they're a real strange lot,
They run around the house all day stuffing themselves -
With chocolates and crisps and still being able to scream and yell!

And the really strange thing is that -
I'm pretty mad but I'm the sanest one of the lot!

Louisa Goodison (11)
The International School of Lausanne, Switzerland

I CAN'T WAIT

I can't wait to grow old and stop working,
To sleep and rest all morning,
To watch my favourite television programmes with my friends
And not have to worry about my business meetings.

I can't wait to grow old and be able
To take vacations whenever I want
To be free to spend time with my grandchildren.
Instead of ugly tight suits and sunbathe on the beach all day long,
Brown and wrinkled as a handsome young man.

I can't wait to grow old and be proud to celebrate
My ninetieth birthday accompanied by my entire family.
Receiving the presents which I now have time for.

I can't wait to grow old and be able to say
That I survived all those tough years of marriage,
Children and responsibility without too much difficulty.
A survivor, washed up by life's tide, beached but content.

Florian Fahrny (14)
The International School of Lausanne, Switzerland

CIGARETTE

In a box I wait,
Waiting to be chosen,
Craving to destroy another life,
My friends have been taken,
and never seen again.
I know they have sacrificed
their lives
To shorten a human's life.
We laugh at the human race,
For we take millions of
lives a year.
Yet they do not learn
that we are the tools of cancer.
The hand comes down
to fill their addiction
for our succulent
nicotine.

Martin Adamson (13)
The International School of Lausanne, Switzerland

I AM OLD

(The voice of a native
American elder)

(Voice of an old man in a
retirement home).

I am old
I have seen the passing of many
Chiefs and generations.
I reflect upon many things;
The wars I have fought in
The people I have seen
The horses I have ridden.
I am wise,
I am respected by all.
People do my bidding
And I am fed.
My needs are supplied
By grateful hands
People come to me
And request advice
About their problems
My advice is always treasured
I have endured many winters,
But the next will probably
Be my last.
I do not regret this for
I am getting tired.
I have accomplished a lot
In my time and
I reflect upon my deeds
With pride.

I am old
I have seen the passing of many
Presidents and generations.
I reflect upon many things;
The war I have fought in
The people I have seen
The cars I have driven.
I am old
I am avoided by all
People ignore me
And I am fed,
My needs are supplied
By hands paid to care
People come to me
To chat and talk
(mostly about the weather).
All my stories are old news
I have endured many winters
With the help
Of central heating.
I do not think
This will be my last unfortunately.
I look back over the years
Which have passed, and
Reflect upon them
With regret.

Mathieu Jones (14)
The International School of Lausanne, Switzerland

WRINKLES TO ME TELL A STORY

Growing old is transforming yourself
You start to get wrinkles,
Wrinkles, wrinkles and even more wrinkles.
Some people have plastic surgery to try and hide them,
But me, I'm proud of having them.

Wrinkles to me tell a story
They are a part of me,
They make up my face.
If people didn't have wrinkles,
You would never be able to tell apart the young from the old
And the old from the young.

Wrinkles to me tell a story,
They are life-lines.
Each one tells a different adventure which I have lived in the past,
Each one is a different path which I have taken in life.

Wrinkles to me tell a story,
Those around my mouth record the different lovers I have kissed
And the jokes I have laughed at,
Those on my forehead are engraved by
The exams I have struggled through.

Wrinkles to me tell a story,
And I am proud of the life they proclaim.
I never would want to be wrinkle-free
Free of life's joy and pain.

Wrinkles to me tell a story,
So read my face and discover my life.

Nadia Bonjour (14)
The International School of Lausanne, Switzerland

REMEMBRANCE

It was never like this when I was young
Now blazing eyes
And searing mouths are weapons.
Instead of the
Blazing guns
And searing fire streaking through the water
From a torpedoed tanker.
And the hunt
Once for a U-boat in the frozen seas
Of Hitler's war,
But war still lives
A war of words
Too dangerous a conventional war
They say
Enemies become friends and the world moves on and
I go out and watch young children playing
And remember how it was
I've seen death,
That grinning skull
With scythe blade shimmering,
He points to the world
And we all tremble
I know that death is always near
Many of the men that served
Under me have walked with the skull,
Their bones litter the Atlantic floor,
But when I die
I want no box in the earth
Bury me in the sea I have always loved,
And let me there meet old friends,

So that I may mingle in death
As I did in life.
And send my spirit high
To meet my crew
And maybe the ship will be there too.

Michael Thomson (14)
The International School of Lausanne, Switzerland

LIVING IN THE PRESENT

When I was young, I was scared to die.
I enjoyed my life and lived in the present,
I never thought about the future, I was scared to die.

Now, sixty years later, I sit here
I've grown old and ugly.
I use a wheelchair
I can no longer live independently.
My life has become boring,
I have nothing to do.
Sometimes I watch the birds,
But lately they haven't come.
I watch the children playing in the street,
Wishing I could join them,
I have nothing to do, but to just sit here.

When I sit here I think,
I think about my life, my children
And their children.
They still have a whole life ahead of them
I don't, and that's what's on my mind.
I won't live much longer, but I'm not scared of dying.
I want to die because I do nothing but sit here and think.

I want to die.

Sophie Hiltermann (14)
The International School of Lausanne, Switzerland

I WILL NEVER KNOW

My face mirrors the past,
Every line on it,
Maps an unforgettable experience,
But have I experienced it all?
I have done so much,
I have brought up my children,
Standing by them all the way,
And minded my loved ones,
But is it enough?
I will never know.

In the back of my mind,
There is always the feeling,
That I have missed something,
Made the wrong choice,
Taken the wrong path.
I abandoned my career,
To care for my children,
Who I rarely see,
But did I sacrifice too much?
I will never know.

I know there is no point,
In dwelling on the past,
But did I take every chance,
And every opportunity?
Should I have chosen love,
Over my security,
And gone with my instincts?
I don't think so,
But what would life be like if I had,
I will never know.

I have been around the world,
I've seen many different things,
I have seen pleasure and pain,
Poverty and plenty, war and peace,
More than many people my age,
But have I seen everything?
Have I achieved everything I wanted to?
If I rewound the time,
Would I do things differently?
I will never know.

Sarah Abery (14)
The International School of Lausanne, Switzerland

THE SPELL OF CREATION

I am the Universe
And within that Universe there lies a solar system
And within that solar system there lies a sun
And around that sun there spins an Earth,
And on the Earth there grows a tree
And in that tree there's born a blossom
And from that blossom there is a seed
And within that seed there burns a fire
And in that fire there burns a spirit
And in that spirit there rings laughter
The laughter rings within my mind
And in my mind there starts a creation
And from that creation there's born a soul
And in that soul there dwells a heart
And from that heart there releases joy
And from that joy there comes no evil
Which rejoices freedom!

Sophie Secker (11)
The International School of Lausanne, Switzerland

MY LIFE TODAY

My life today is not much fun,
In fact it is a boring one.
Every morning I wake up and go to the bathroom,
Which I cannot do, without someone holding my hand.
Yes, you halfwits, I am old,
But for God's sake leave me my dignity.

I have all day to read the local newspaper
About events I will never take part in.
The closest I will get is sitting in my old rocking chair
In front of the television screen.
My 'helpers' give me 'no-spill' cups to drink from!
I am just old,
I am not a goddamn idiot!

I feel I am trapped,
I want my freedom, and I want my fun.
Instead of taking my medication
I want to go game hunting in Africa.
I want power over nature.
Instead of a trip to the doctor I want to go skydiving
With the wind whipping through the sparse grey hair left on my head,
Giving me a rush to last me for the rest of my days.

Instead of dying a boring death, I think
I will make a big scene in Paris.
Yes, I will climb the Eiffel Tower
And I will gather everyone's attention
And right before I jump off,
I will think to myself that some old fart
Will read about me in the local newspaper and
Marvel at my last words:
'My life today was a lot of fun,
But now my time here is over and done.'

Juandré Posthumus (14)
The International School of Lausanne, Switzerland

WITHERING AWAY

As the ages accumulate,
As the wrinkles cover me,
As my mind dies,
As my hair goes shiny grey,
I look at myself in the mirror
And watch he younger me wither away.
I used to be handsome
Not a decrepit old mess,
I used to have friends
Always ready for a laugh,
Not arthritic old men
Playing chess with trembling hands.
I used to be up-to-date, á la mode,
Or even up-to-beat, as some would say,
Not some unfashionable, old-fashioned
Geezer in a rocking chair.
I used to have fun!
But now I am old,
Now I am boring,
Now my own amusement
Is watching the years pass.
Will you remember me
For what I was?
Will you spite me
For what I have become?
Or will you treasure and love me
As you would a newborn child?
I pray you will at least accept me
Before I pass on.

Adam Gradwell (14)
The International School of Lausanne, Switzerland

A GOOD DAY

Today,
Nothing worthy happened, but not anything of sorrow,
The sun is shining, the rain is falling,
The water's glimmering, a sailboat passes by,
Today was a good day.

Met a new person, saw an old friend,
Read a long novel, enjoyed a tasty meal,
Didn't do anything, just stayed home in bed,
Watched the sun set, ending a good day

Cried all day, can't anymore
'No' was echoing in life today,
And it didn't go the right way,
It seems like the worst thing I the world, but it's not,
It's still a good day.

It's a good day,
In a good time,
In a good chapter,
Of a good life.

Michael Battalia (13)
The International School of Lausanne, Switzerland

IT

It . . . with spots of blue and black,
Its hair all up it looks back,
It spies on me as I approach,
I carry on carefully.

It . . . has bright red fangs,
It could rip me apart with two big bangs,
It is now approaching me,
I back off cautiously.

It . . . is jumping with eyes of red,
It pounces on to my bed,
It growls dangerously,
I scream loudly.

It . . . is now ripping me apart,
It spots my heart,
Its eyes roll with joy,
It is the end for sure.

David Naylor (13)
The International School of Lausanne, Switzerland

ATOM TERROR

As the horizon darkened
Night fell upon the world
That was when good turned to evil
The first nuke has been dropped
Dracula has come out to play
Evil has come out of slumber.

The new art of war has been introduced
People flee and
Buildings crumble.
The mighty explosion is over half an hour long

Now it's time to suffer from the poison gas.
It's not safe to go anywhere
It's not safe to yell
It's not even safe to breathe.
The people who survive
Years later die from gas poisoning.

Jack Mirza (11)
The International School of Lausanne, Switzerland

THOUGHT FOR THE FUTURE

When I turn sixty-nine
I'll drive a futuristic sports car and
Burn down the freeway at two hundred and ten.
I don't want to wake up in the morning
With a bad taste in my mouth
In the back seat of a rusty old car
Abandoned on the sidewalk.
I want to party every night until dawn breaks at six.
When I turn eighty-three
I don't want to sit in a home watching TV soaps
Drinking tea with all old geezers,
Moaning about young people today.
I want to drive down Beverly Hills in my Ferrari
Picking up jogging chicks
Taking them out to dinner.
And when I turn one hundred,
Let lightning strike me dead!
I don't want a heart attack,
To linger in a hospital
Hooked up to a machine,
Waiting for someone to pull the plug.

José Marques (15)
The International School of Lausanne, Switzerland

NIGHT SKY

All I see are endless fields of colour
A thin line of clouds form
While the air is still crisp and light
As the deep dark blue sea
Begins to emerge and
You can see no more

Suddenly the shimmering stars appear
One by one perfectly placed
Finally the last fingertips
Of the sun fade away and
You are left with the beautiful fullness
                              of night.

Alessandra Battalia (11)
The International School of Lausanne, Switzerland

A STALLION DREAM

Standing at the top of a towering cliff
majestic and alone
you can see a magnificent stallion
blending in with all the snow.

On a spur of a moment
he jumps from the cliff
and gradually I can see
the horses playing in the mist.

They gallop down swiftly snow flying up
hooves barely touching the ground
they move so fast and surely
they hardly make any sound.

I follow them through the evening
and into the night
while an eagle from her nest
jumps up into flight.

The night-time sky gets lighter
the stallion rears and fades away
into a dream that can't come true
in a land far away.

Manuela Burki (11)
The International School of Lausanne, Switzerland

PARENTS

Parents I don't understand them,
They seem so nice and sweet,
But if you dare do something bad,
Then they will not be as sweet,
They shout at you and send you to your room,
'You're grounded for a week', they say,
But then forget about it.

Parents, I don't understand them,
They tell you what's right and that you have to behave,
But I tell you this because I know that when you're not there
They act like seven-year-olds,
All the bad manners come when you're not there,
And when you come home and break the rules they shout at you,
I don't get it.

Parents, I don't understand them,
They send you to school to learn what they have learnt,
But when you need help for homework you will see,
That it's not just you that needs education,
They need it too.
'Mom, help me with this, I don't understand,'
'Ask your dad, I don't know, I never learnt that,'
'Dad, I don't get this, help me please!'
'Not now,' he says, 'ask your mom,'

Parents, I don't understand them,
They do all the opposite of you,
And they don't get in trouble that's the worst,
I am sure and will always know that I'll be a much better
Parent than that.

Cecilie Dybwad (13)
The International School of Lausanne, Switzerland

OUR PLANET

A dot?
A blue dot?
But let's look closer . . .

A marble?
A marble so used and worn
That it has scratches all over it.

But let's look even closer . . .
We can't see water inside.

Water everywhere
And bits of clay floating.

What we don't know about this blue dot
Is that it is inhabited by very small creatures,
Crawling like fleas on the surface of skin.

It looks very beautiful from afar,
Yet it is getting greyer and greyer.
Wars, smoke stacks,
Water getting darker and darker,
Hate.

But if we look carefully
We can still find pureness.

The Earth is like us,
Full of life and movement
Although it appears to be so still
From a distance.

This blue dot,
Our planet.

Damian Laird (13)
The International School of Lausanne, Switzerland

I AM

I am the sea, many things dwell within me
I am the sand, friends with the infinite waves
I am the snow, which brings much pleasure
I am the wind that flows between us
I am the clouds that view the world from above
I am the mountain in which my peaks have no end
I am the stars of endless light
I am the desert, so silent and so deadly,
Barely anything can take my hateful wrath,
I am the grass, so wide and so vast
I am the winter, which summons the cold wind
I am the spring, in which many things bloom
I am the summer that spreads warmth like the golden sun
I am the autumn, which paints the world in colour
I am the sky much higher than high
I am dusk and dawn at the same time
I am the moon that fills the world with my silver gleam
I am the sun who rises and sets, leaving behind me a trail of colour
I am the rain that quenches thirst
I am the past, present and future
I am the history, time and infinity
I am the Earth
I am the Universe.

Maxime Iten (11)
The International School of Lausanne, Switzerland

THE MOUNTAINS

The wizened men stand towering over the lake,
their white hair a symbol of their status.
Clothed spectacularly in rocky earthen hues
and a lush green overcoat,
their wrinkles show their age.

But age shall not prevent them from groping, searching,
striving to reach the sky,
nor from looking down disdainfully at the clouds.
And still, a thousand years on
will stand the wizened, white haired men
staring resolutely, powerfully across the lake.

Darren Kirke (14)
The International School of Lausanne, Switzerland

HOMELESS

Cold, very cold
Nothing to eat, nothing to wear
I'm getting old,
But who would care?

They just walk by
They just ignore
They don't even realise it
They have much more.

All of them so happy
All of them smile
None of them know
I've been here quite awhile.

I feel my stomach shrinking
I feel my body shiver
My throat is really sore
I think I have a fever.

Until someone finds me
And provides me with a cosy bed
Until then, I'm going to sit here
And sleep on the street instead.

Izabella Depczyk (13)
The International School of Lausanne, Switzerland

THE ENDLESS CIRCLE

Darkness closes in like a thick fog,
Over the buildings of the town.
Spreading, growing like a living creature,
It rolls, unstoppable, over everything,
In its infinite path.

The only light comes from
A scarlet spot on the far distant horizon.
Its crimson rays flood over the buildings and reflect,
Off windows, like a wash of blood.
The stars are hidden by a blanket of dark clouds.

The clouds part, and a full moon shows,
Pushing a sliver of light down to the shadow-covered land,
Illuminating water to the brilliance of polished glass,
And dousing houses in its silvery rays.
The clouds shift again, and the world sinks into the eternity of darkness.

Dawn breaks the impenetrable dark cloud,
Like a beacon of hope through troubled times,
The sun rises, a huge globe of golden warmth,
Radiating peace and joy for the new day,
Rising to its full height, it basks the world in its glory.

The new sun bathes the world in its endless brilliance,
The light rolls over the peaceful countryside,
Showing the green hills and the sky changing,
From jet-black to jubilant robins' egg blue,
Showing God's creation in all its finery.

And as the grey clouds of dusk make their approach once again,
The world is plunged into twilight,
The people and animals ready themselves,
For the night, as the owls take to flight,
The endless circle begins once more.

Travis Kirke (11)
The International School of Lausanne, Switzerland

OLD AGE AT LAST

Yes! Old age at last.
Finally, I have reached my prime!
No more stress of endless work
No more troubles with my smart, young boss.

I can finally go to the places
I've always dreamt of.
Or spend some of my new-found time
Helping my dearest grandchildren make sense of the world.

When I had a job, the busy world of work and stress
Left no time for living
Playing cards and laughing with friends,
Travelling slowly around the country.
Enjoying the world at last.

No more alarm clock,
Out of the window with you!
Get up whenever I want and be lazy
Or stay up real late, talking into the night.

Who said the older, the more neglected you get?
I can live on my pension
Even waste a few coins at casinos and dog tracks.
With my health at its peak,
Old age rules! It's not what you think!

Freddy Kwakman (14)
The International School of Lausanne, Switzerland

MY TRUE LOVES

A soft, velvet blanket stroked against my cheek,
The overwhelming sweet scent of fresh flowers,
The powerful aroma of steaming banana bread,
Creamy Swiss chocolate melting on my tongue,
A big, juicy turkey roasting in the oven,
Soft blueberry muffins like magnets, pulling me towards them,
Birds musically chirping a melody,
Water racing to the beach from far out,
Untouched, glittering snow resting so peacefully;
The damp smell of the earth after it rains,
The grasshoppers disrupting the calmness of the night,
Laying in the cool green grass on hot summer days,
Water trickling down a stream,
A rainbow-coloured sunset over the mountain peaks,
Motionless, calm pools gleaming clear as clean glass,
Evergreen Christmas trees covered in shiny tinsel,
Moonlight shining down onto the sea.

Kelsey Picken (13)
The International School of Lausanne, Switzerland

PROUD OF MY WRINKLES

One day a curious child will ask me for the two digits
That most elderly people hide as their deep, dark secret
I will answer that I am over that hill and in the valley gladly
The street will be my catwalk
My chin will always point towards the sky with pride
Unlike all of my friends,
I will not get a surgery to reduce my smile lines
The smile lines will show how many times I laughed

Most people regard sun spots as ugly signs of old age
They will remind me of lazy days spent on the beach
And the good times I had under the sun
My hair will not be turning grey
To me, the grey will be beautiful streaks of blonde
When my two digits begin to near three,
I will not hide the signs of ageing
I will be proud of my wrinkles.

Sarah Ingram (14)
The International School of Lausanne, Switzerland

THE DEADLY CHASE

He was running,
Running away from them,
Running away from the mad men.
He knew why they were chasing him,
He knew very well why.
He had stolen their plans to steal the Queen's crown.
He clutched the valuable papers in his right hand,
And he was sprinting at great speed.
They were catching up,
He knew they were, he could sense it.
They had flaming torches and pitchforks,
And he came to a large gorge,
Too far to jump.
They were closing in on him,
So he leapt with all he was worth,
Only to plunge to his, bloody death.

Michael Topp (13)
The International School of Lausanne, Switzerland

I WISH I WERE, BUT I KNOW I AM

How do you want me to be?
I am weak,
I can hardly walk.
I breathe and chew and sit.
I wish I were sportive and happy,
Healthy and quick-minded.
When I was a little kid I wished I were older,
But now I . . . I wish I was younger,
In those days all I thought of was my hunger.
I wish I were exciting,
Fascinating, daring, a party-loving person.
Now all I am no longer what I was.
Now all I was is turned upside-down.
I am a slow, weak, grumpy, unhealthy,
Lonely, sad and slow-witted.
All I do is sit in my chair
Waiting to lose all my hair.
I don't know where I belong,
For how long do you think I will go on?
I'm becoming absent-minded and don't know
Where to hide.
I do fear my death, I want to die,
And then I can lie in my bed.
Then I can wish - wish all I want and
See my old pal Fred.

Tim De Nijs (14)
The International School of Lausanne, Switzerland

WISHING

In my rocking chair I sit,
Looking at the door,
Waiting for a knock,
Or a nice friendly hello.
I would like to know I am loved.

Beside the crackling fire I dream,
Of the many wonderful days I have.
Wishing for my youth to return to me,
Enabling me to do whatever I want.
I would like to be young again.

Before the television I sit,
Looking through thick glasses,
Staring into a world no longer of my own,
But into a world I longed to be part of.
I would like to have fun.

On my creaking bed I sleep,
Dreaming up fantasies I long to live.
Perhaps one day,
You never know.
I will be back on my own two feet.
Just you wait and see.

I wish . . .

Nicole Wong (14)
The International School of Lausanne, Switzerland

THE MOUNTAINS

The mountains are higher than the sky,
As I look at them I sigh.
When the sun sets over their peeks,
Water trickles down and leaks.
Into the lake so big and blue,
Around the trees, and through and through.
I can sit and stare for hours,
Through the sun and late May showers.
Down by the lake at night,
Little mosquitoes like to bite.
In the morning when the sun rises,
The mountains are big surprises.
In the summer the mountains are green,
In the winter they can clearly be seen.
In the fall they seem to reach high,
In the spring they seem to fly.
In the summer, winter, fall and spring,
The mountains are the most beautiful thing.

Jared McKnight (14)
The International School of Lausanne, Switzerland

THE CENTAUR

The blue eyed creature looked sad.
She had red hair and a blue body.
Walking under the full moon
She suddenly saw a fire
The nearer the fire,
The more she heard a strange music

Behind the mountains,
The sun (like a red ball)
Rose in a purple sky.
A cry of joy,
And she was gone.

Justine Egloff (11)
The International School of Lausanne, Switzerland

THE BOOK

On the shelf
In my room
There are some shells
And also a book.

It is red
With golden letters.
I eat bread
Whilst reading the letters.

I read and read
Reading all of it,
I sleep and sleep
Thinking about it.

Matías Jaques (11)
The International School of Lausanne, Switzerland

SAND IN AN HOUR GLASS

Slowly, it leaves.
Each day a little more,
It slips away
Like the sands of an hour glass.

It started when I went into a room
Full of purpose
Then forgetting why I went there.
I would sit,
Thinking so hard,
Trying to remember . . .
But nothing.

Then I forgot my street.
I stood there for hours,
My mind a riddle
I could not solve,
Forgetting where I live
My home for the past sixty years.

Slowly, it leaves.
Each day a little more
It slips away
like the sands of an hour glass.

Now days are a blur
The bad days outnumber the good.
They tell me on bad days
I cannot even recognise
My own children.
I shout at them to leave my house
As cruel intruders.

My brain is dissolving
Before my eyes
Without explanation or reason,
Without a cure or response.

I am left powerless
My inevitable end in sight.
I will sit in a home
With glazed-over eyes,
Rambling on about the past
In another world
Trapped in my mind
All on my own.

Recognising no one,
Knowing nothing.

Slowly, it leaves.
Each day a little more.
It slips away
Like the sands of an hour glass.

But that is then
And now is now.
Yet I can't help but think and fear
When will the sand in the hour glass
Run out,
What then?

Brittany Berryman (15)
The International School of Lausanne, Switzerland

FROM SOUL TO SOUL

I stand beside my window late at night
And through the vast, incalculably far
Distance of space, my eyes receive
The signal of a gently pulsing star

This light has journeyed through a billion miles,
Through icy darkness, lightness, barren spheres
Of emptiness from very far distance of space
Across who knows how many thousands of years

A comic message that has found its way
To me at last its terminus eyes
Your soul and love that I need so much
And what I know I won't ever give up

Perhaps it grieves the stars to be alone
This grieves for us like for the stars to be alone
The fact that they can never meet again
Through night, through ice and through emptiness

Oh star why do you weep? You are no
More isolated than our love for each other
Not more than the earthly spirits, dwelling at removes.
Through distance cannot separate us never.

Who is to say which is the further off
The stars from each other or our love?
Nobody can tell us what is further,
But our love is waiting forever and will be
Together forever and ever.

Alexandra Palotas (18)
The International School of Naples

FRIENDS

Friends forever, these are the words,
That can give us the whole world.
Side by side, walking together,
Nothing comes between us, never!

You listen to me, anything I say.
You advise me, properly, every day.
I can hear your words and fears.
I am here to wipe your tears.

In my happiness you celebrate with me.
When I'm sad, by my side I find thee.
When you laugh, the sun brighter shines.
Your sadness makes darker the skies.

Any problems are nothing against us.
walls we face, crumble to dust.
Against the wind we always run.
With our friendship we can fly up to the sun.

Our friendship goes beyond countries and creeds.
Nothing stands between us.
You are for me and I am for you,
Someone special.

And that's what real friendship is *forever.*

Fivos Paschalis (17)
The International School of Naples

Something Special In My Heart

I want to talk about a girl
I want to show that she is
Something special in my heart

I cannot say her name
I cannot say her age,
But with two words or less
I'm going to describe her

Her behaviour was divided
In sun and moon
In day and night

Every time that I see her
I feel something special in my heart
Something that is telling me
That I love her

Here I expressed
All that I can say
Because in another way
You will know who she is.

Pablo Gamundi (17)
The International School of Naples

Dreams

As the night rolls in,
and the sun begins to hide,
I start to feel the tingling
of my conscience wanting to rest.

As I lay down,
and shut my eyes,
my mind goes to places,
that with feet you can't arrive.

Through adventure and fear,
happiness and love,
I said through my dreams,
never wanted to awaken.

A world of dreams,
where you can do what you want,
it depends on your imagination,
and how you let it flow.

Andreas Fernandez (15)
The International School of Naples

PERFECTION

We always look out for true beauty,
Wanting perfection in all we do.
Who put the definition for such a word?
The meaning itself is too great.

The seven wonders of the world!
Only seven?
Who decided on those?
Is true beauty seen by all or one?

Look around outside!
Why make things perfect when they already are?
I mean natural beauty is so great
There's no need to build, as buildings destroy one's views.

Wanting is needing,
Needing a source so great
Why look for something?
We have so much,
But never know where to look!

Rahila Esposito (15)
The International School of Naples

MY FRIEND

When I saw you the first time,
I hoped you would follow me through my whole life.
Now, when I wake up every morning,
I see the face of my friend.
You are sitting next to me when I read,
or when I do my homework.
I can tell you everything,
and you will always keep it secret.
Every day when I return from school,
you are very happy,
you start jumping high and running around me.
When I go outside, you follow me,
you would never run away or be mad with me.
I've known you for nine years,
and you have stayed the whole time with me.
In the night you sleep next to me,
and make me sleep well.
You will always stay my friend,
even if the world should end.
We are friends and no one can separate us.
You are my friend,
even though you are different:
I am a girl and you are a dog,
but you'll always be my best friend.

Cathrin Kusche (13)
The International School of Naples

A WINTER NIGHT

On a winter night
A white man runs
A snowman
With a pipe
A snowman
Chased by cold
He runs to town
Where he goes into a house
To warm up
He sits on a stove
And all that remains
In a puddle
Is the wooden pipe
And an old snowman's hat.

Femke Tol (12)
The International School of Naples

WHAT'S WAR . . .

What's war?
If not that feeling of hate and revenge which lives within us forever.
What's war?
If not a man who goes out to die for something he does not believe in.
What's war?

If not all the thousands of white crosses that remain in our hearts
forever and remind us that someone is not here anymore.
How many innocent have died fighting for something they were
too young to know, something that had been decided by a God who
is no longer in heaven?
How many families will cry their loved ones who did not come
back from hell?

Andrea Salvia (15)
The International School of Naples

WEATHER MAN

As I look in the sky,
a dark gray sky,
a feeling of sorrow
washes over me,
just like the rain that begins to fall.

A chill up my back
from the whistling wind
blows my happiness away,
just like the last few autumn leaves.

A frigid cold in the air,
freezes my joy,
just like an icicle.

My emotions are swept away by the weather,
just as the fog rolled in.

Jason Woods (16)
The International School of Naples

IMPRESSIONS

Both pointers show the vertical.
Outside it's dark and silent.
The wind waves some clouds over the moon.
The stars so blank, so shiny.
So far away but within reach.
The darkness fears me, it is cold.
Upstairs millions of little eyes look at me,
Take care of me, I feel safe
If I look up to the sky, my imagination goes on a journey.

I see the Pegasus, impressive, sliding over the firmament,
It passes the Virgin, by the Scorpion.
Soon the first sunbeams chase away the eyes.
It becomes light.
The moon goes and the eyes close.
They look forward to the next sunset.

Sandra Berthold (17)
The International School of Naples

MISS COCAINE

Soft, pure and white,
but really hard to fight.
Fascinating, tempting and strong,
till the end you don't know that is wrong.
When you meet her she makes you feel good,
but as soon as you leave her you get a bad mood.
You want her, you need her, you are two souls in one,
although she's so evil and death she'll make come.
Who is she? Where is she? Now we all know,
Miss Cocaine is her name, gotta let her go.

Laura Lubrano (18)
Vienna International School

THE SOUNDS I HEAR

I hear . . .
The sound of birds chirping in the morning.
The engines of ferocious cars starting.
The silent sound of children awaking.
The noisy, angry, horrible sound of machines starting.
All is awake, all is noisy.
The sound of a cat miaowing for yummy food.
The noise in my mind thinking one billion things at a time.
The annoying noise of my sister trying to find her French book.
Chairs squeakily pulling out for breakfast.
Noise is the sound we need.

Laura Griffin (11)
West Island School

FRIENDSHIP

A friend is someone who holds you tight,
When something isn't feeling quite right.
A friend is someone who knows how you feel,
When something you're scared of is suddenly real.
A friend is someone who feels your pain,
When thunder and lightning are in a sky of rain.
A friend is a person, who is nice and kind,
You were that person I was lucky to find.

Lucy Griffin (11)
West Island School